SAFARI FOR SANITY

Phil Gray

ISBN: 978-1463674359
ISBN-13: 146367435X

DEDICATION

To Donna Mae

PHIL GRAY

ACKNOWLEDGMENTS

Special Thanks to Marge Porter, Barbara Coles, Melinda Wilson, John Wilson, Ann Bernson and David B Casey.

1

Before – Honolulu, Hawaii, early 2008

It was a tough year. I was a defendant in a nasty, lingering commercial lawsuit that just wouldn't go away. It was a maddening lawsuit, the kind that deprives you of your money and fiddles with your sanity in the process. I had just endured a grueling deposition that challenged my faculties of civility and had been a hair's breadth from leaping across the conference table and pouncing upon the opposing counsel when my attorney laid a calming hand on mine, pulling me back from the brink.

An earlier time when I felt similarly unhinged I went on safari to Tanzania and climbed straight to the summit of Kilimanjaro, the highest peak in Africa at 19,340 feet. Physically, that was the most strenuous exercise I have ever undertaken and it nearly dealt me a knock-out blow. The adventure was exquisitely consuming, however, and it quickly took my mind off all else. By the end of it, I felt completely restored and so inspired that I wrote a humorous non-fiction book about it (*Kilimanjaro via the*

5

Marangu Route, available at Amazon.com). But that was years ago, 1996. I call that Safari #3 because I had been on safari in Kenya and Tanzania twice before. And then in 2003, I went to South Africa for the first time for a mixed-bag adventure we might call Safari #4. So by my calendar and frame of mind, a Safari #5 was not only long overdue, it was essential to check the unwarranted intrusion upon my sanity. Moreover, I could best accomplish that by loosening the few reigns on my sense of humor and reporting the experience. Hence these pages.

Giddy now with a plan, I checked the small globe I keep prominently displayed in my bedroom for just such an occasion and discovered that Namibia is on the opposite side of the planet from my home in Hawaii, give or take a few degrees. Aha, I thought, a capital starting point. Namibia represented the most distance I could put between myself and the stupid lawsuit, literally as well as figuratively. A twofer.

I'm an Africa buff. Safaris are my particular passion. Mention the word "safari" and I get animated and vociferous. Otherwise I'm as dull as a box of hammers.

Dictionaries describe the safari in its narrowest sense as a trip to Africa to see wild animals in their natural habitat. This, I think, is the modern version of the word now that the hunting safari is politically incorrect and universally frowned upon. I prefer the modern version.

A hundred years ago I might have thought it very cool to go off to Africa with Teddy Roosevelt and shoot up the continent, killing four-legged beasts as fast as I could load the gun. But I'm a 21st Century guy, wouldn't hurt a flea. Worse, I'm a vegetarian.

The point of killing animals for sport is patently absurd anyway. There is nothing macho about taking bead on an innocent antelope and punching him dead.

And most assuredly, I've never wanted a dead head on my wall, fake eyeballs staring down accusatorily, asking why I shot him in the first place. I've seen the real thing, the frightened eyes, the tense pose. He's scared to death. And well he should be. *What's that human want with me*, he's thinking. *Dude don't belong here; he must be up to no good.* He's wise to think that way. He gauges me warily, keeping a safe distance before bouncing off across the savanna, skittish and quite alive. Maybe I'll capture him on film and maybe I won't, but at least he'll be alive and his mate will be happy.

After ten trips to Africa, five of which were Sub-Saharan, a funny thing happened to my appreciation of the safari: I came to see that there is far more to it than images of wild animals fixed in the mind's eye or caught on film. The word is more elastic than that. It allows for a wider range of travel adventure. It evokes the exotic, unknown, untamed continent, and hints of inconvenience, maybe hardship, even danger. The Kilimanjaro climb is an example. Although its principal objective is not to film animals and it is a form of sporting event, it is an endeavor conducted in the African wild, on foot amongst its inhabitants. It is very much a safari.

On the adventure scale, the modern safari ranks beyond *hike*, and just before *spelunk*. The first cousin of a Himalayan *trek*.

The discussion is incomplete without mentioning that a companion is a crucial ingredient of the safari experience. If you don't have a companion, I say don't go.

The safari was made to be shared. Failing that, it is sadly hollow. When you witness your first kill, you will instinctively cry out, "Holy crap! Did you see that?" Also instinctively, you will look around for confirmation. And you will feel pretty stupid if no one else is there. Besides, there is nothing more intimate than the startled grasp of your companion when the low guttural moan of a lion floats over the cool night air, ruffles the tent, and awakens her. That, my friends, is sharing a moment.

My companion is my dear wife, Donna Mae, the self-appointed boss of me. She hadn't given a thought to the continent of Africa 40-something years ago when I talked her into marrying me. At that time she had dreams of indulging her wanderlust in a more genteel continent, one noted more for its wine than its wildlife. But she was sport enough to follow my lead and we've had a jolly good time of it. And, I must say, she has become her own kind of genuine Africa buff. Africa will do that to you if you let it.

In short, the safari is what you make of it. It can be (or can include) a personal journey of discovery, or rejuvenation, escape, penance, or a voyage of friendship and camaraderie. Or it can be just a lark.

Most safaris are the latter, a simple holiday, a damn fine lark. And indeed in the past I have always considered them as such. I make no excuses. But sometimes that kind will fool you, will transcend the paradigm, touch the heart, pose unanswerable questions, and linger.

We had to go back for a Safari #5.

It would start out as just a lark.

Our story is best begun with a synopsis of Safari #4.

2

Synopsis of Safari #4 – South Africa, 2003

We headquartered at the Pretoria home of Melinda and John Wilson, American friends who have lived and worked in the public health industry all over Africa for more than 30 years. The Wilsons are genuine American heroes, for reasons that will become evident later. For now, suffice it to say, we go back a ways. (Amongst other fond remembrances, my Kilimanjaro climb had been with John Wilson and two Wilson sons.) Part of this safari would be just Donna Mae and I, and part would be with Melinda and John.

Donna Mae and I began by flying to Port Elizabeth and self-driving the Garden Route down along the Indian Ocean coastline to the Cape of Good Hope, thence to Cape Town. South Africa is a vast and rugged country, none of it more stunning than this stretch of its south-eastern coastline, fractured and whipped to a chilly frenzy by year-round southeasterly trade winds.

It took some doing to enjoy the view though. We had an unfamiliar rental car and I was obliged to drive it on the wrong side of the road, a taxing challenge even in a vehicle with an automatic transmission. But ours had a manual-shift, operated by the left hand, seated in what should be the passenger seat. Attempting this for the first time implies a death-wish and requires prestidigitation. I had neither and still we managed to survive.

Our first stop was at the coastal town of Knysna, a picturesque holiday spot exceptionally popular amongst affluent South Africans. After perusing the trendy shops and scarfing a lunch at a pier restaurant, we drove a few clicks to the main attraction of the Garden Route, Tsitsikamma National Park. It is a national treasure: a pristine wilderness of mountains, valleys, rivers and forest occupying 80 kilometers of coastline on the Indian Ocean.

We found a parking lot at a clearly-marked trailhead and hiked through dense forest, down a rugged mountainside and across slippery streambeds to an unspoiled rocky beach. As we were making our way casually through the woods it occurred to me more than once that there are infinitely more unfriendly critters living here about than you might find, say, in the placid forests of the California Sierras. I'm not embarrassed to admit that this observation put a bit of an edge on our little stroll. After a few minutes, I mentioned my concern to Donna Mae who was leading the way mindlessly *un*concerned. "Pussy," she barked over her shoulder without looking back or breaking stride.

Sharing your inner-most thoughts with your wife is always risky.

On the beach, we stood open-mouthed in awe. Angry surf pounded on an inhospitable agglomeration of jagged boulders, worn stones and dirty sand. So unlike the tidy white-sand beaches of Hawaii, so stunningly beautiful in its own right was this tableau that Donna Mae wanted to take a piece of it back home.

"Pick something small, dear," I begged.

After some considerable prevarication, she selected a grey stone the size of a grapefruit. It was worn smooth as a baby's ass by several millennia of unceasing tidal forces and she insisted I carry it home in my pocket.

"You're kidding?" I said.

"Nah! It's not that big," she answered dismissively. "In an alternate universe it's just a grain of pixie dust."

Who can argue with that logic?

It is now on a shelf in our study, prominently displayed like a Fabergé egg.

Continuing on towards Cape Town, we decided it would be sinful to pass so close to the famous town of Stellenbosch in the heart of wine country without dallying for a few days at a ritzy-titzy winery hotel. It was there – of all places – I got to handle my first cheetah.

Downtown Stellenbosch was unremarkable, plain as white-bread, hot, dusty and contained nothing to make one want to linger there. So we did not.

The winery hotel we found on the outskirts of town, however, was just the opposite. Set on a vast open site with wide pastures and stands of trees following beside a tiny river, it boasted no more than 50 rooms. There were several barns with stables for horseback rides and the winery's shop stocked to bursting with its wares. The hotel was a single two-story structure, its architecture a minimalist, random arrangement of bone-white, flat-planes, all set at right angles to each other. The structure was warm and inviting despite its visual severity and was clearly designed to make its guests thirsty.

The place had an attraction one might call a wild-animal petting zoo, which I could no more avoid than a kid could a carnival. And since I would not be driving any more that day, I was free to sample the winery's wares. Succumbing to the subliminal effects of the clever hotel architecture, I did so with impunity. By the time of my visit to the cheetah enclosure, I had enough of a buzz on to approach the event as an hilarious yuck.

A man-size lady wearing safari garb and a menacing expression ushered me into a fenced pen, whispering, "Don't make any loud noises or quick movements." She was about to add, "or I'll rip your dick off," until I feigned submission, signaling that I got the message.

A large adult cheetah was stretched out on the ground, reclining peacefully. Bored probably. Another stern young lady in safari garb knelt next to the cheetah, keeping a firm grip on the collar about its neck and appraising me suspiciously.

Nice pussycat, was on the tip of my tongue but something about the body language in the pen suggested my particular humor would not be appreciated so I refrained from unleashing it.

Sensing that I was going to be a civil chap, the handler-lady said, "You may touch it carefully if you want."

I bent down on one knee and ran my hand slowly along the cat's pulsating side. I was amazed at the taut musculature of its shoulders and imagined their immense power, the principal attribute that makes it the fastest land animal on the planet.

The cheetah eyed me warily but never shifted position, unnerving me more than if it had.

By the time this brief encounter was over, the two ladies were guarding the faintest of wry smiles and I had lost the buzz.

Here was one of the differences – I was to learn many more – between the safari experience in East Africa (Kenya & Tanzania) versus that in Southern Africa (South Africa, Namibia, Botswana, Zimbabwe & Mozambique). In East Africa, you don't touch the animals; you don't even get near them. Things are looser in Southern Africa.

As if to confirm that, we got very near a male baboon the size of a linebacker at a rest stop on the road to the Cape of Good Hope. He was sitting on a wall scratching his nuts and watching us warily as we walked to the restrooms. A ranger was busy admonishing a family of tourists to put away their picnic lunch and get back in their car. He said the scratching of nuts was just a distraction. The wily baboon was actually eyeing their sandwiches, getting ready to make a dash for one. Then he laid on the punch line: "He's got very sharp claws, and if you happen to be biting into your sandwich when he snatches it, he will take your lips with it."

That's all the admonition I needed. I did the green-apple-quick-step in and out of the restroom and back to our car.

In Cape Town we stayed three nights at the Cape Grace, a five-star hotel of outrageous luxury. It sits prominently at the entrance to the famous Victoria & Alfred Waterfront, arguably South Africa's major urban tourist attraction. The first two days, we enjoyed the shopping, the restaurants, and the cable-car ride up to Table Mountain, getting the silly things out of the way before taking the hydrofoil out to Robben Island on the last day.

The notorious island prison was officially closed in 1991, and now sits as a stark reminder of South Africa's shameful apartheid years. Most of the guides are former prisoners, able to put their pain and anger sufficiently aside in order to shine an educational light on a sad chapter of the human spirit that should not be repeated.

Our guide was an elderly gentleman who had been incarcerated there for thirteen years. He was exceptionally polite, though obviously not cheerful, as he took a small group of us through the prison compound. It was cold, bleak, and fiercely depressing. He showed us the kitchens, gang toilets, group dormitory, and outdoor exercise yard, finishing the tour at the cell where Nelson Mandela was imprisoned for 18 years until public opinion forced the apartheid government to move him to alternative incarceration on the mainland. That humanitarian gesture lasted eight more years.

Another guide, a much younger man, then took us in a small bus to see the gravel pit where prisoners with hand shovels had been made to toil in the hot sun while armed white men stood guard over them.

Nearby, within earshot of the pit, was a row of dog kennels, strategically placed so the animals' savage snarling could be appreciated by the toiling prisoners. The dogs were not needed for tracking; the island is small as a postage stamp and the closest land is more than four miles away over shark-infested waters.

Although this guide was a child during the apartheid years, he still understood the depth of depravity behind the kennels' purpose and he let his passengers know it. His briefing was polite and articulate without being deferential, fairly raising some eyebrows amongst those in the group I figured were Afrikaners. But those were the eyebrows of those who had it coming. I admired the guide his pluck.

We were somber in the hydrofoil on the way back to the mainland. Back in the sixties, the expression for that kind of a chilling experience was *heavy, man.*

I looked over at Donna Mae. She was quietly watching ocean spray misting the boat's windows, no doubt reflecting on our tour. I knew she was thinking the same thing I was thinking.

"Heavy, man!" I said.

She nodded agreement.

The requisite Cape Town experience behind us, we then flew back to Johannesburg for a few days before commencing our six-day, self-drive safari through Kruger National Park with Melinda and John Wilson.

But first – because this was our first time in South Africa – Melinda wanted us to have a proper tour of Johannesburg. She had arranged a car and driver to show us the important sites so off we went...eagerly, I might add.

The driver was an articulate and affable African chap who seemed to have a wealth of experience illuminating white folks to the realities of South Africa.

The first stop was in Soweto, the incomprehensibly dense shanty town, known the world over for its squalor and disregard for human habitation.

After winding through a thoroughly depressing area, the driver pulled up to a small building, more a hovel than a house. It was a rectangular conglomeration of boards and sections of wood with a flat roof of tar paper weighted down with stones. An elderly lady emerged, smiling kindly, and the driver introduced her as "Mama." She greeted us warmly and showed us into a small sitting room that was neatly kept but claustrophobic due to a low ceiling and very little light. The floor was bare earth covered by various pieces of carpet, and in the middle of the room a kettle steamed quietly, moisturizing the air. Against one wall was the kitchen: shelves with dishes and pots and a flat working-surface the size of home-plate. No cooking implements were in evidence, nor was there a table to sit at. The other walls were covered with colorful pages from popular magazines, lacquered or so it seemed to legitimize them as wallpaper. The effect was more legitimate than one might expect and reeked of dignity. There were few items of furniture so we did not sit down.

The driver followed us in and handed Mama a bag of clothing and a bag of food items Melinda had given him for her. She smiled more broadly at that and thanked him in a language I did not recognize. Then she offered us tea, which we declined knowing it would only dilute her bare stocks if we accepted. The driver said something in the language again, apparently indicating it was time to go, and she beckoned us to follow her out a back door to her garden, occupying a corner no bigger than a bathmat. She gestured proudly at an unfamiliar assortment of herbs growing in gallon cans. Although thin and scraggly and clearly lacking water, the plants appeared carefully tended. The driver explained that Mama was a traditional healer and used these plants in her practice. Further, he said, she was a doctor, respected in the neighborhood as such and consulted often. I looked at her just in time to catch the hint of a knowing smile cross her face and *gotcha* rang silently in my pea brain.

In the next tenth of a second I realized the magnitude of the honor bestowed upon us to be received by this revered lady in her home.

We left humbled and unprepared for the next stop, the monument to the famous Soweto Uprising that had made headlines worldwide in 1976.

The Uprising started as a student march, a peaceful protest of the apartheid government's new law requiring the Afrikaans language to be used in all African schools. This was seen by Africans as a further emasculation of their identity. It was the last straw.

The march had been carefully planned by a handful of students, but word of it spread quickly and hundreds of other students joined spontaneously. The police were mobilized to maintain order and things soon got out of hand. A number of students were shot and killed, first among them a teenager named Hector Pieterson. A photo of the dying Hector being carried in the arms of a friend, Mbuyiswa, became the iconic photographic image of those worldwide headlines. This photo is emblazoned eight-foot high on one of several black granite tablets and is the centerpiece of the monument that bears Hector Pieterson's name.

As usual at noteworthy African sites, a dozen or so craft stalls stood nearby broiling in the hot sun. Donna Mae was perusing the crafts while I sat on a granite bench regarding the monument. After several minutes she returned with information that quite unsettled me.

"That boy's mother has one of the stalls," she said, pointing to Mbuyiswa on the granite tablet. "She sells postcards with that photo on it."

"What?" I said stupidly. "You talked to her?"

"Yes! She said he was wanted by the authorities after this photo appeared in all the newspapers and so he left the country immediately."

"Did he return?"

"Never did."

I did the math. "That was thirty-three years ago. And she never saw him again?"

"That's right. And she only heard from him once, a couple years later, and he was afraid to reveal his location even to his own mother."

"Jesus Christ!"

So ended our tour of Johannesburg.

In South Africa, local white folks prefer to safari in their personal vehicle, self-catering their meals, snacks, and beverages. The tourism infrastructure is nicely set up for that. All but the most absurdly luxurious game reserves and bush lodges have kitchen facilities for self-catering. Many campsites also do. BushBaby trailers are the popular conveyances for hauling the implements of safari, the food, drink, clothing, camp chairs, binoculars, cameras, cook stoves, charcoal, torches, deet, etc.

This part of our safari would be with Melinda and John Wilson.

John had rented a BushBaby and so we loaded it up with our stuff and set off late on a Friday afternoon...for the bush.

Our principal destination was Kruger National Park, but before entering we stayed two nights at a private game reserve adjacent to the park called Tshukudu Bush Camp. Tshukudu is a "Big Five" (lion, leopard, elephant, rhino and cape buffalo) game reserve on 5,000 hectares of private land. Our accommodations were one-room stone huts, clean and comfy, one per couple. In a small clearing between the huts we set up our camp chairs and a small table. Security from visiting critters was provided by a single wire, waist-high, presumably electrified, strung around the encampment. We had our evening drinks there, content in the bush, wishing for nothing more.

The first morning, a cheerful ranger-type named Bob, armed with a rifle, took us and four other guests on the one-mile walk in the bush down to a water hole to meet the resident elephant family. In the pre-walk briefing, Bob said, "There will be a baby about five feet tall, a tame mother, and a wild father. It's okay to touch the baby and the mother, as long as you don't make any threatening movements that would excite the father." Bob did not elaborate on precisely what a wild bull elephant might consider threatening, but it was obvious to the dullest tourist that anything more than *tentative caressing* would be foolhardy.

Ranger Bob also said he was bringing two "friends" along on the walk. One was a sleek adult cheetah, and the other a 13-month-old lion cub the size of an Alaskan malamute. Both animals tagged along with us like common house pets. We were encouraged to fondle the cheetah carefully, Bob claiming it was domesticated. He further claimed that cheetahs are the only cats that can be domesticated. True or not, Donna Mae said we could not have one.

Bob said it was okay to pet the lion cub too, so long as we did so warily and not too chummy because it had been trained to be released into the wild next month. John and I took turns patting it on the head gingerly so we could say we fondled a lion. The womenfolk weren't having any of it. Women are superior to men in that respect.

The second morning we went on another walk to the water-hole with the same group. This time Ranger Bob brought two different "friends," a full-grown adult leopard and its handler.

The handler was a stocky ranger-type wearing a sidearm.

The leopard bounded about freely, tracing wide circles around our group.

"Here's the deal with the leopard," Ranger Bob said sternly. "Keep your eye on him at all times. Always know where he is. Whatever you do, do not turn your back on him. They kill by striking at the back of the neck, you know."

More than one set of bowels in the group loosened with this news.

We took Bob's advice as gospel.

Although I felt we had become old hands at walking in the bush, the leopard gave the morning an exciting tension, one missing yesterday.

While we continued on towards the water hole, the leopard bounded off into the bushes and circled back again. Round and round he darted, several times, paying no mind to the lot of us, or so it seemed. All the while, the handler shadowed him like a cop on a pickpocket.

Eventually the leopard wandered over to our group and stopped on a low mound about ten feet away. He looked us over imperiously, as if he'd been trained to pose…or was hungry.

He just happened to be between me and Donna Mae.

"Get closer, Donna Mae, get closer," I said, fumbling for the camera.

All we have of the incident is a fuzzy shot of her giving me the finger with a leopard in the background.

The next day, we visited the Moholoholo Wildlife Rehab Centre, a non-profit that cares for injured, abandoned, and poisoned wildlife, principally lions, leopards and cheetahs. These are animals that could not survive in the wild due to their condition. They are cared for at Moholoho and – to the extent possible – bred for the release of their offspring back into the wild. There is no touching or fondling at this place.

We were invited to a short briefing on the subject of vultures, a feature I thought somewhat incongruous with the mission of the place. I was soon disabused of that impression. Vultures are the good guys, the janitors of the bush. They clean up after everyone else has had their repast. Rotten and decayed tissue is to them what steak tartar is to us. Thus they consume the most repulsive faire, maggots, worms, bacteria and viruses, thereby cleansing the landscape for Mother Nature's next go-around. They have a bad rep because they are so ugly. This is unfair.

They are not nearly as ugly as a Pekingese dog and they are useful to the environment which a Pekingese is not.

Properly briefed, we were invited into the cages to hold some vultures. Donna Mae would have none of it, but I went. The handler fit a leather arm-cover stretching from fingers to elbow onto my outstretched arm. Upon my arm he placed a vulture about the size of an eight-year-old with a wingspan of six feet. The beast's claws dug into the leather arm-cover fixing him tightly to my arm. He looked at me – not menacingly, just with annoyance – and flapped his wings in my face. Something was not right. My quivering was apparently an impertinence, at which time the handler placed a pole under my arm steadying it.

Thereafter, the vulture and I were able to enjoy a few quiet minutes of bonding. Even so, it was quite unsettling to stare into the beady eyes of a critter that can pluck your eye out faster than you can blink. Assuming vultures are not inclined to do that sort of thing, wouldn't one make a good house pet? Imagine the clean-up job he could do around the yard. And he is not a predator, only a scavenger, so you don't have to worry about him killing your little Fluffy. But if Fluffy got run over by a car, he would promptly circle overhead to show you where you could find her. And should you wish, he would clean her up for you for a dignified burial. Is that not a handy pet?

We left Moholoholo with a full appreciation of its stewardship of endangered species and a firm belief that its dedicated personnel are amongst our modern heroes. As the planet shrinks from the inexorable encroachment of human habitation into wildlife habitats, animal species are becoming extinct at an alarming rate. Rehab centers and wildlife conservation camps fight to slow this process. It is an unsung effort.

I was feeling warm and fuzzy in a newly-purchased Moholoholo tee-shirt until I was informed that the reptile farm was our next stop.

That was John's idea, not mine.

I'm about as interested in the subject of snakes as I am in quilting.

In truth, I hate snakes. Such is my dislike of snakes that I wrote a whole book on the subject once. Some would call that an obsession. Au contraire! I think it quite healthy. It's Alice Cooper should have his head examined, not me.

We pulled into a small dusty parking lot next to a round, low-walled, muddy pit containing an inert crocodile the size of a submarine. Beyond the pit was a drab, one-story brick building containing dozens of glass cubicles housing every kind of serpent native to Africa. At the entrance to the building, a lady with a wide smile collected a small fee to go in it. If there was anything I didn't want to pay a fee for, this was it.

If you didn't want to pay to see the snakes, you could stay outside and watch the croc for free, which was like watching grass grow. It was either the oldest croc in the world or made out of concrete. I thought about poking it with a long stick to find out, but Donna Mae gave me that don't-even-think-about-it look, so I didn't. Instead I made faces and called it names but still it did not respond.

Crocs are like that. Wily bastards! They can remain in one position for hours, fooling their prey into thinking they're dead or asleep before striking in the blink of an eye. It's frightening to see. Especially if you're the prey.

Somebody paid the small fee for me and we went inside the snake building. We were met by an older man wearing soiled work clothes and holding a cage full of mice. "Welcome friends," he said with a grin. "You're just in time to watch me feed the snakes."

Oh perfect! Just what I wanted to hear.

The man beckoned for us to follow him into the bowels of the building where I endured an hour of watching snakes swallow mice. Snakes are compassionate creatures. Some snakes first anesthetize their victim with a quick bite before swallowing it. This thoughtful act is to spare the victim the ignominy of being awake as it is gulped down the snake's gullet in slow agonizing jerks. The spectacle reminds one of humans eating raw oysters.

After I got over the revolting part, it became boring.

I began to fall asleep on my feet when the man reached into a larger glass cubicle and extracted a six-foot-long python. This was not the kind that eats mice; this was the kind that eats pigs and goats.

I back-peddled smartly to keep from messing my pants.

With one hand the man held the python tightly just behind the head so it could not bite him, and with the other hand he held it away from his body so it could not squeeze him. The thing was angry and coiled around the man's arms.

24

"You want to hold it?" the man said.

"Sure," said John.

"Not in this lifetime," said I.

Donna Mae and Melinda disappeared as if they'd been vaporized.

John held the python and I stood well back so he couldn't throw it at me.

All afternoon I had been wondering what we would be having for dinner, but this episode with the snake put me off food and on Stoli for the night.

Our last nights on safari were inside Kruger National Park. The first two nights were at the Oliphants Restcamp in a luxurious house on the edge of a steep cliff overlooking the Oliphants River. The house was surrounded by a high chain-link fence, electrified to discourage the baboons from visiting. A thousand feet below, we watched elephants, buffalo, giraffe and kudu sharing the river testily with its massive crocodiles. Large black eagles wheeled in the thermals high above, scouting for lunch.

Christ, it was magnificent there.

I hoped it would never end.

But of course it would; the next day was our last. At a snail's pace, we drove in a southerly direction the remaining length of Kruger Park, pausing occasionally to snap photos of the wildlife. The longest pause was about an hour to allow a herd of a hundred or so elephants cross the road from right to left. "Cross the road," is a loose term here; actually the elephants dithered about the road, dining leisurely on the foliage that bracketed it, eventually engaging more foliage on the left side than on the right. In that sense, an hour later, they had crossed the road. Elephants are impervious to any schedule but their own.

We spent the last night in the park at Pretoriuskop Restcamp where – it was rumored – a lady tourist had gone strolling about the campgrounds one balmy moonless night and got herself eaten by a leopard.

In a Spartan but comfortable bungalow, we had our last safari dinner together, toasted our good fortune, and did not venture out.

It was with these fond recollections in mind that Donna Mae and I went back in March 2008, back to safari with the Wilsons once again, to explore more of South Africa, and to widen the itinerary this time to include Namibia, Zimbabwe, Botswana and Swaziland.

3

Safari No. 5 – 2008

Johannesburg, South Africa – 2 days, preparation

We arrived at OR Tambo International Airport in Johannesburg during a Wednesday afternoon rush-hour after a tiresome but uneventful 17-hour, overnight flight from JFK. Melinda Wilson collected us and whisked us back to their house in the upscale, Waterkloof district of Pretoria, a half-hour drive from Johannesburg.

A party marking the commencement of a proper safari starts upon arrival at the first venue – in this case, safari-headquarters at the Wilson house – regardless of day, time, or the travail of getting there. And so it did.

As soon as our bags were in the door and the two dogs had sniffed us down, John broke out the sundowners, cheese and crackers. In the flurry of arrival chatter, Melinda pulled together a light dinner and served it on the open-air patio just off the kitchen. It was the last week of the rainy season and the air smelled of dampness, but the night was warm and we were finally in Africa. All the rain in the world could not have dampened our spirits.

We killed a couple bottles of fine South African wine, and discussed the plans for our Namibia departure until the booze and fatigue bade us goodnight.

The next day, Melinda and John went off to work and Donna Mae and I checked out the house and the neighborhood.

Pretoria is the capital of South Africa, and Waterkloof is the Beverly Hills of Pretoria. Virtually every home in the neighborhood consists of a two-story main house with a garage, servants' quarters, and manicured yard, all surrounded by a high wall topped with electrified razor-wire. The Wilson house is one such, built of classic red brick, the architecture tending towards an English motif. The interior is furnished tastefully with a mixture of very fine pieces, predominantly traditional European and contemporary African.

Maggie is their full-time, live-in housekeeper. Tall, statuesque, 20-something pretty, and almost bashfully reserved, she floats through the house with quiet efficiency, keeping it spotless and uncluttered. Back in her hometown of Polokwane, 130 miles north of Pretoria, her mother cares for her young child, whom she might visit once a month. Jobs are scarce for unskilled workers in South Africa and it is not uncommon for many to incur extraordinary inconvenience, even hardship, to secure a position and hold onto it. Maggie's situation is obviously not ideal for a young mother, but her employers are generous and thoughtful, so she is one of the lucky ones.

There is a live-in yardman, Thomas, age 37, waif-thin, and no more robust than a 16-year-old. He is HIV positive, kept alive by an antiretroviral drug regimen arranged and paid for by the Wilsons. *Kept alive* that is, if he takes the meds as directed and resists the efforts of a traditional African healer who tries to convince him to reject the white man's magic. Thomas struggles with this conflict of cultures and is slowly paying the price. Around the house, he is like a ghost (no pun intended), quiet and scarce; I saw very little of him in the five weeks we were there. When able, which are most days, he keeps the grounds tidy, the dogs groomed, and John's Toyota 4-Runner immaculate.

At night, an armed guard patrols the grounds outside the walled-compound, sharing his duties with two adjacent houses. Every home in this section of Waterkloof has similar security. In front of the smaller homes, the guard can usually be seen reclining on the ground with his back against the wall, a weapon of some kind in his lap. At the gated front entrance of the larger homes there is usually a small guardhouse the size of a phone booth– which is difficult for the guard to recline in, but not impossible.

The Wilsons' two dogs patrol the grounds inside the walls. One is a large, all-white German shepherd, so soft and beautiful everyone wants to hug him all day, and the other is a grisly, midsize Boerboel pug, so ugly only Donna Mae wants to. Both animals are deceptively friendly, with hair-triggers trained to discourage unwelcome visitors.

The Wilson house is a delightful place to be a *welcome* visitor.

4

Namibia – 10 days, self-drive, rental car

Friday afternoon, Melinda, John, Donna Mae and I flew from Jo'burg to Windhoek, Namibia's capital city, located in central, though unspectacular, grassy highlands. Windhoek is small for an international capital city, relatively uncongested, and tight enough to walk around its downtown in an hour, although there is nothing much to see. The city's most striking feature is the number of wide main boulevards named after popular revolutionaries.

A tall, scruffy guy with *Wilson* scrawled on a piece of cardboard stood waiting for us when we arrived at Windhoek International Airport. He loaded the four of us and two lady travelers into a large van and drove 45 minutes into the city to find the cozy B&B Melinda had booked for one night. We assumed the guy was from the car-hire company where John had booked a 4x4 SUV for our self-drive safari, but it turned out he didn't know squat about our car-hire arrangements. He had just been sent by someone to pick us up at the airport. And he wasn't clear about who the someone was who sent him either.

But before finding our B&B, he had to drop off the two lady travelers at a downtown hotel and, in the process of doing so, promptly got the van stuck under the low ceiling of the hotel's parking structure. John and Melinda – old hands at life in Africa – bolted from the van as if it were on fire, leaving Donna Mae and me to assist the driver in freeing the van.

Watching the backs of John and Melinda disappear on the run through the exit of the parking structure, I said to Donna Mae eagerly, "Where'd they go; where'd they go?"

"To find a Spar Market," she answered, as if I were a half-wit, "to buy a cooler and fill it with snacks and drinks and ice. Where do you think?"

They must have been talking about that at some point during the ride into town, but apparently I missed it. You miss a lot of shit when you're old and deaf.

With the collective brainpower of the driver, Donna Mae, and me, we managed to get the van unstuck by the clever trick of removing the luggage rack.

Free at last, I realized we had no idea where we were; we had been in the middle of this remote African city for all of fifteen minutes, thirteen of them in the parking structure. We had a clear idea *why* John and Melinda had taken off, but no idea whatsoever *where* they had taken off *to*. And the driver was no help; he was still rattled from getting the van stuck and by having two of his passengers flee the scene. The poor guy was *non compos mentis*; his contribution to our dilemma had deteriorated to looking befuddled and picking his seat.

Rather than search on foot, I badgered him into circling the block with the van. After a few rounds I spotted a small sign that read *Indoor Mall*. "Pull over," I cried, startling him. As his knee-jerk reaction slowed the van, I jumped out and ran into the mall.

At this, he was either more rattled or had become immune to his passengers' precipitous departures and in such a state that he blithely pulled to the curb at an odd angle, turned off the ignition and followed after me.

Donna Mae took off after him, wishing neither to be left alone in the van nor left out of the fun.

Things had happened so fast it never occurred to me – or anybody else – that we had left our luggage in an empty, untended, unlocked van, illegally parked on a main thoroughfare, in the middle of friggin nowhere.

And I thought the driver was *non compos mentis*.

Meanwhile, deep inside the mall, I came to a glass-railed mezzanine that overlooked a dazzling Spar Market. Next to the glass railing, sitting on a bench as if waiting for a bus, sat John and Melinda.

Beaming triumphantly from a successful shopping spree, Melinda smiled. "Oh good!" she said, with a little clapping gesture. "You found us."

Donna Mae and the driver caught up huffing and puffing to find us laughing like teenagers.

Then it dawned on me.

"Uhhh, who's with the van?" I asked.

Donna Mae glared at me while the driver muttered something to himself that sounded like Elmer Fudd saying *ba-dee, ba-dee, dats all folks*.

"You left the van with all our shit in it?" John asked, directing the question at me.

The driver let out a sigh of relief.

"Oops!" was all I could muster.

Then we turned on our heels and charged back through the mall, laughing hysterically.

The driver wasn't sure whether to laugh or cry.

Back in the van, our possessions were untouched.

I waited.

Sure enough!

"Nice going, birdbrain," from Donna Mae.

"You were the last one out," I countered lamely.

"What was I supposed to do? You left me alone."

"Children!" barked Melinda, and now we all laughed so hard we cried.

By now the driver was showing early-warning signs of hallucination, so Melinda called for calm and dug out her directions to the B&B. Naturally, we navigated by committee, arguing about directions, endangering pedestrians, and further unsettling the driver. But in spite of these obstacles, and to his credit, he managed to get us to the B&B without mishap. No amount of further questioning, however, elicited an iota of additional information regarding who had sent him or our car-hire arrangements for the next day. I think his nervous system was shot.

We had a long drive ahead of us in the morning so we wanted some assurance that our car would be ready and that we would be able to get an early start. John worked his cell phone impatiently until he found a warm body at the car-hire company and was able to express his consternation with the dearth of information forthcoming from the driver.

Apparently John was persuasive; at 8:00 in the morning, a cute little blond girl in tight jeans stood waiting for us in the B&B parking lot.

"Good job, John," I said.

Donna Mae poked me in the ribs.

"Can't be many of them in Namibia, eh?" I whispered to John.

A harder poke in the ribs.

The girl was all business. She had a different van and took us to the car-hire place where she signed up John for the 4x4 Nissan SUV he had booked. We loaded it up with our stuff, and by 9:30 we were finally heading due north on Namibia's National Highway No.1 for the six-hour drive to the Etosha National Park, spitting distance from the Angola border.

The road was relatively flat, straight, empty, and paved.

They don't say "paved" in Africa, they say "tarred." Few roads are tarred in Africa outside of cities and populated areas. When you are on one, you rejoice.

On the outskirts of Windhoek we encountered a government roadblock serving as a loosely organized checkpoint. We slowed to a stop, a couple of armed, uniformed gentlemen (it was not clear if they were police or military) looked us over, said not a word, and waved us on. Neither was the point of the checkpoint clear. It seemed to be of a permanent nature so it hadn't been set up quickly to apprehend some fleeing criminal. Maybe some citizens, for some obscure Namibian reason, were just not permitted to leave Windhoek. A similar checkpoint was operated in the opposite direction and I wondered about the opposite premise.

The whole thing took less than a minute and we continued on our way scratching our heads. The harmless unfathomable vagaries of Africa are an indispensible part of its charm.

As we continued north, both sides of the road gradually became overgrown with thick unruly vegetation, mostly bushes and small trees left largely in their natural condition. Here and there a cottage or small farm poked through. After a half hour, the landscape became virtually devoid of human habitation, became an emerald palette, unspoiled and pristine.

After about three hours, we stopped at the small town of Otjiwarongo for petrol, snacks, and more ice. Donna Mae, Melinda and I were in the station's convenience store for half a minute when a fire alarm went off and Mammy Yokum burst out of a back room screaming at the top of her lungs and chased everybody out and locked the door on the inside. That seemed counterintuitive to me, and when the door stayed locked for too many minutes even after the alarm ceased screeching we went across the street to a Spar Market for our provisioning.

The market was gigantic, bigger than a Whole Foods Market and every bit as well-stocked – right there in backwater Otjiwarongo? This tidbit of information is worth remembering when you are on safari in the middle of nowhere.

Although for a different reason, I would also remember the armed security guard stationed at the large opening at the front of the market through which shoppers of all colors were both entering and exiting. He was a large uniformed black man and he stopped and frisked every black man that exited, but he paid no mind to any white folks. We could have carried away a cash register.

The centerpiece of the Etosha National Park is the *Etosha Pan*, a huge natural depression, 1837 square miles of silt and clay sediments forming a flat beige pancake in the dry season and a shimmering silver lake in the wet season.

The *Etosha Pan* is the central attraction of the Big Five and multitudes of lesser mammals, birds, and reptiles. It is the chief tourist attraction of Namibia.

The Pan is oblong-shaped, about 70 miles long east-to-west, and about 40 miles across. Along the southern side of the Pan, there are three 4-star resorts, Namutoni, Halali, and Okaukuejo, spaced equal distances apart and linked by gravel tracks. These are the only resorts *inside* the Park and, as such, are much prized. Melinda had booked us into each one for a night.

Nearing 4:00 PM, we checked into the *Namutoni Resort* on the eastern edge of the Pan, another place seemingly in the middle of nowhere. There was a modest stone reception building set apart from twenty or so individual bush chalets grouped together and linked by raised wooden walkways.

The chalets stood next to an old German fort, white-washed to a blinding white and refurbished to include two restaurants, a bar, and several curio shops.

Out behind the fort, towards the Pan, there was a night-lit waterhole for game viewing. Warthogs dashed about the grounds for no apparent reason, running under the walkways and disappearing into the bush. It was hotter than a pizza oven and very thirsty out.

The chalets were new, elegantly appointed, and air-conditioned. Each had a stylish bathroom with a deep tub, double lavs, and an outdoor shower inside a fenced privacy patio. They were ostentatiously luxurious, and somewhat inconsistent with the main reason we had come to the *Etosha Pan*: to see the wildlife. But I saw no reason to lodge a complaint with the management.

In the morning, we finally got down to the business of game-viewing, popping the top of the 4x4 and heading westerly towards Halali along the gravel track skirting the southern shore of the Pan. The landscape to our left was lush with the scraggly brush and acacia trees preferred by the larger mammals – rhino, elephant, and giraffe – herbivores *least* concerned with predators. On our right, looking north towards the Pan, the terrain was less dense, with a smattering of brush dotting the wide open fields preferred by the herd mammals – springbok, kudu, impala, oryx, zebra, wildebeest – browsers *most* concerned with predators. These lesser animals manifest their concern by a predilection for safety in numbers and an abiding affection for lines of sight. Humans should learn from this.

The Pan was immense. Looking farther north, it stretched to the horizon, hazy and indistinct. There was no far shore to be seen, only the end of the earth, as if confirming that it really is flat.

Ordinarily, the shoreline of the *Etosha Pan* teems with wildlife, on a par with *Kruger Park*, the *Serengeti*, and the *Masai Mara*. But it was the tail end of the wet season and there had been so much rain that pools of water were everywhere and the animals had no need to crowd the shoreline. Wildlife, therefore, was not *abundant*. But that is a relative term in Africa. There is always *some* wildlife.

The gravel track made the going slow, and perfect for game-viewing from an open top. Standing on the back seat two at a time, arms resting on the rooftop, we took turns enjoying the best vantage point for spotting wildlife and luxuriating in the gentle caresses of warm safari air.

We spied plenty of kudu, oryx, springbok, Burchell's zebra, warthog, giraffe, ostrich, and the odd wildebeest. The Big Five had no need of the Pan and were not to be seen, but it wasn't our first Africa safari so we were not bummed.

At Halali that evening, no animals came to the waterhole, but at dinner in the open-air restaurant a slick, black-backed jackal the size of a golden retriever sauntered by our table looking for scraps. I was momentarily startled to see a jackal so close but quickly recalled that in the Sierra Nevada Mountains of California we learned not to feed the coyotes. That knowledge suggested a parallel premise: no good can come of befriending a jackal.

We left him alone.

The next day we drove toward Okaukuejo, the third and last *Etosha* resort. Finding the route sparsely unattended by wildlife, we continued north beyond Okaukuejo to a barren place on the western edge of the Pan called Okondeka. Melinda said there was supposed to be rhino there, but there was nothing except thick mud where the Pan kissed the shore and a pink smudge on the horizon to the northeast.

There was no wildlife apparent in the immediate vicinity so we stopped at the edge of the Pan and had a sauvignon blanc lunch and took photos of each other standing on a monument that read *Dangerous Animals – Do Not Get Out Of The Car*.

John was fascinated by the pink smudge on the horizon. "There's something out there," he said.

"Nah! You're seeing things," I said. "It's a sauvignon blanc mirage."

John checked it out through his binoculars. "Holy shit!" he cried, "Flamingos."

We got out our binoculars and, sure enough, there were hundreds of thousands of pink flamingos, standing blindingly brilliant in the late afternoon sun, so stunning it made our day. The number, "hundreds of thousands," may seem like a careless exaggeration but a little research will tell you it is not. Flamingos of that magnitude are commonplace in Tanzania's Ngorogoro Crater. Even bigger numbers belong to the wildebeest and zebra in their annual migration that starts in Kenya, loops south into Tanzania and in late summer flows northeast out of the Serengeti into Kenya's Masai Mara. The wildebeest number between 1.5 and 1.8 million, depending on their location and time of year. The zebra are an integral part of this migration and their numbers range between 300,000 and half a million.

Backtracking to Okaukuejo on a little used gravel track, we found ourselves in the middle of a massive herd of impala using the track as their main thoroughfare. They were content to allow us the privilege of traveling side-by-side with them so long as we did so quietly and at their speed. We were happy to oblige. After all we were merely visitors in their town, unlike the few odd warthogs that darted in and out amongst them like uninvited cousins deficient in social skills. This is not to suggest that warthogs are unwelcome in such context. Quite the contrary, they are not only welcome, they are indispensible, a neighbor-species' contribution to the vigilance that is innate and constant where predators are concerned. This is also why you see the wildebeest seemingly happy to have the zebra tagging along on the migration.

Returning to our rooms from dinner that night with Melinda and John, we crossed a wide green lawn that opened to an immaculate, starry sky. John pointed out the famous Southern Cross, high above and seen almost exclusively in the southern hemisphere. There, almost alone in that particular patch of sky, prominent as if no other celestial objects existed, twinkled four stars forming a small cross with short arms and a longer stem. The cross lay on its right side in the aspect of a wooden cross set down on the ground. An imaginary line drawn from left to right across the arms of the cross and followed downward almost to the horizon led to an extraneous fifth star. The imaginary line and the fifth star, John explained with proprietary enthusiasm, point due south, imbuing the Southern Cross with a critical navigational attribute relied upon for centuries by ancient seafarers and explorers.

Donna Mae and I were floored. The obvious prominence of the Southern Cross was a startling revelation. One is almost embarrassed to have been ignorant of it. But once we had beheld it, un-obscured and brilliant, on a cloudless, moonless African night, we were tagged. And it became etched in our memory bank, a permanent part of our ken.

We left the *Etosha Pan* early the next morning and drove five hours south and west to Swakopmund, Namibia's premier ocean-side, resort town situated on the Atlantic coast and surrounded on its other three sides by the empty Namib Desert. One's first impression upon arriving at this man-built oasis was succinctly expressed by John as we hit the first traffic light: "This place has no business being here."

But the Germans thought it did, a little over a century ago after the Dutch and the Brits had scooped up South Africa and the Portuguese had grabbed Mozambique. If someone had to grab another piece of Africa, I was happy it was the Germans. We enjoyed two nights at a small, immaculate European-style B&B, walked about the clean comfortable streets, marveled at the German colonial architecture, shopped for native crafts, and dined in splendor on windy piers jutting into the choppy Atlantic.

Swakomund was quite regular as oceanfront resort towns go. As regular as Cape Cod or Venice Beach. What wasn't quite regular, however, was the family of three lounging in the grass at a small park. They were all painted red, head to toe, red as a Washington apple.

Himba.

Perhaps the last remaining, truly semi-nomadic pastoralists are the Himba people of Kaokoland, a wild mountainous area occupying the far northwest corner of Namibia. The Himba live off of their cattle and goats, following along as the animals search for good grazing. They travel on foot with all their worldly possessions wrapped in animal skins. This is not particularly startling to those familiar with the similar lifestyle of the Maasai people of Kenya.

What is startling is that the Himba, unlike their Maasai cousins, paint themselves red, head to foot. They cover their entire bodies – skin and hair – with a paste made of butter, ash and red-hued ochre. It is a primitive form of suntan lotion and also protects their skin from the harsh and unforgiving climate of Kaokoland.

Just when you think you might be the great world traveler, wise and unflappable, you discover the Himba. And while trying to maintain your cool you eat a large serving of humble pie.

Of course, the Himba family didn't know that and wouldn't have cared if they did. They sat quietly in the grass, enjoying the warm sunny day, communing only with each other. They were beautiful. Majestic.

"Is there a custom here?" I asked John? "Should we exchange greetings? Offer money?"

John shrugged. He didn't know.

"Guess I'll mind my own business," I mumbled.

There was no air of supplication in their countenance to suggest any contact was sought. They were in a state of grace, as true to themselves and their identity as is humanly possible. But that is not surprising; it is their way. Neither were they seeking, nor did they need, anything from us.

Himba.

So we continued on, leaving them undisturbed.

"Did you see that, Donna Mae?" I said, as we walked away.

"See what?"

"Proof they don't need anything from us."

"What proof?"

"Dude had a cell phone."

Leaving Swakopmund in the morning, we drove south through Walvis Bay, heading deeper into the Namib Desert towards our next destination, the Namib-Naukluft Park. Consisting of almost five million hectares (the size of Costa Rica), the park is the third largest in Africa. It is the home of Sossusvlei (try that on a couple of martinis), a vast expanse of desert consisting of spectacular, towering red sand dunes and miniature dry pans.

I remembered one guidebook claiming the Namib Desert is "generally believed to be the 'oldest' desert in the world," at about 80 million years old.

"Holy crap," I thought. "Drive on, John," this I gotta see.

Fifteen minutes outside of Walvis Bay, the tarred pavement gave way to the gravel track that would be our principal thoroughfare for the next three days. The track climbed up into broken hills, wound through rugged ravines still raging from recent rains, and traversed precipitous mountain passes before descending southwest onto endless gravel plains and high desert.

After about four hours, we rolled into a lonesome place called Solitaire, a dusty desolate rest-stop and campsite that was once a farm. Our guidebook said the place derived its name from the lone dead tree in front of the petrol station, but it seemed like everything else was dead for miles around, so the name of the place would have been the same without the tree.

As I looked around at the endless expanse of dried scrub and rocky soil baking in the heat, soft winds kicking up tiny dust devils, I was compelled to wonder whose bright idea it had been to start a farm there. And what could it possibly grow? The farm was doomed from the start; that should have been obvious. But don't blame it on the tree; it was just the messenger.

There was a rustic open-air restaurant with a half-dozen people seated under a canvas shade that provided scant respite from the sweltering afternoon sun. The guidebook said the food was good there, but the temperature far out-weighed taking that chance.

I went into the ramshackle sundries store – the only other place where there was shade – and noticed a plate of homemade apple fritters displayed on a beat-up counter. I was hungry and they looked mighty tasty so I seriously considered buying one. I began waving the flies off them when a giant cook the size of Haystack Calhoun oozed out of the kitchen. He was wearing a sweat-stained, wife-beater undershirt bulging with tits bigger than Dolly Parton's. I thought I was going to be sick.

But he fooled me.

"Hi there," he said, with a bright smile. "Welcome to Solitaire. What can I do for you today?"

"Haven't quite decided yet," I said, caught dumb again.

"Well take your time, sir," he continued amiably. "It's hotter'n Hades out there and there's no need to rush things, especially when you're here in the shade."

"Thank you," I said, meaning it.

He offered his hand, saying, "By the way, my name's Clyde." And even though I knew that giant paw would be hot and sweaty, I shook it anyway, saying, "John."

Surreptitiously wiping my hand on my shorts, I stood amazed at the odd contrast between the man's personality and his physical appearance. I couldn't help liking him.

We chatted a bit further, about where we were from and where we were going. In the end, I found him to be so perfectly charming he could have sold me the whole plate of fritters if he'd been covered in a burka. I finally settled on a couple bags of potato chips and some cokes and left the place muttering to myself, something about judging a book by its cover.

An hour or so later, sometime in the late afternoon, at the end of a long descent from the high desert, we cruised into Sesriem, the world's smallest town. It consisted of a one-pump petrol station, a room passing as a "market," a tourist campsite, Park Headquarters, and the Park Gate where I adopted the night-watchman two days later.

Sesriem is a blip on the map and is little known. The general area is more popularly known as Sosussvlei.

Adjacent to Sesriem, was the 5-star *Sossusvlei Lodge*, simmering innocently in a 120-degree Fahrenheit cloudless sky. We checked in for the two-night stay Melinda had scored.

Twenty-six newly-built, individual bungalows sat pristine on the desert floor, fanning out thirteen on a side from an immaculately tended reception area with a restaurant, bar, and pool. The structures were a symphony of smooth clean stucco planes, softened by an ochre palette that mitigated their intrusion on the desert floor.

A few miles away, there was a more expensive lodge, consisting of eight, individually air-conditioned, super-luxury units, advertised for those to whom money was no object. How silly, I thought. Our bungalows had a tented roof over the sleeping area, a ceiling fan to move the hot breezes, and an immaculate ensuite bathroom. And, of course, we had our cooler full of beverages. You just don't need more than that; if you do, the Namib is not for you. It is not a place for sissies. In fact, most of Africa is not for sissies…but I digress again.

We were bone-tired from the day's drive, but not yet done. Melinda said we had to drive inside the park and see the famous Dune 45 at sundown. Coincidentally, Dune 45 lies 45 kilometers from the Park Gate. Melinda is the acknowledged expert in matters of safari lore so there was immediate assent from all hands. At the hotel bar we replenished the ice in our traveling cooler and set off.

The road *inside* the Park was paved. We hadn't expected that, but it was a welcome respite from the bone-jarring of the gravel tracks we had just spent the day on. A bigger surprise, however, was finding the road bracketed by immense sand dunes, living mountains of fine-grain sand, sediment from inland rivers that flow into the sea much farther south. The sediment is washed up on shore by the tides and is dried by the sun and lifted and carried northeasterly by prevailing winds blowing off the Atlantic Ocean. The dunes of Sosussvlei are only a small part of a larger system of continuous dune fields that begins just south of Walvis Bay and extends some 300 miles farther south as far as Luderitz.

In morning light the dunes of Sosussvlei are shades of beige and ochre and maroon. In the setting sun they are red. But not the blood-red of the Himba, rather the fire red of the dawn of creation.

We were there at just that time of day: sunset. All the dunes were the same startling, fire red. When we arrived at Dune 45, it was the reddest of the red, and stood as high as a 10-story building. It was shaped like a door-stop, the long plane on the right to windward, the shorter steeper slope on the left in the lee.

Sosussvlei dunes are the highest in the world, ranging in height from 600 to 1,000 feet. The crest of Dune 45 is one of the highest. Its surface was hot, smooth, and shifting, ever so slowly. The air was very hot, and very dry. Thirsty air.

We broke out the vodka sundowners and toasted our friendship and great good fortune. Then we toasted Melinda for another perfect score.

John, Donna Mae, and I started up the dune. Warm sand filled our shoes. Large black dung beetles scurried to avoid us. A soft wind blew clouds of fine particles over the crest. Halfway up, Donna Mae and I quit and went back to the parking lot to work on our sundowners with Melinda. John continued to the top to have his picture taken.

Back at our bungalow, there was just enough light left to see an immense herd of springbok grazing on the plain in the distance to the east and two ostriches pecking away at the ground a hundred meters off to the west, outlined by the setting sun. The ostriches were still there later when we had dinner on the open-air patio facing the plain.

Next morning we set off on the key adventure: the drive into the Park to the Sosussvlei after which the area is generally known. Sosussvlei is a dry pan (*vlei* means pan), surrounded by smaller dunes and hiking trails, usually kept at a soothing 120 degrees Faranheit by the blazing sun. It is marked by a 4x4 car-park located 65 kilometers into the Park, 20 kilometers past Dune 45. Pay attention now, there are important statistics coming.

I had been looking forward to this particular drive for years ever since Melinda first suggested Namibia. I knew it would include the famous Namib Desert. To me, the traverse of even a small portion of any serious desert is incomplete without evocative music. Just as a drive through the Vienna Woods cries out for a Strauss waltz, and a trip through the Rocky Mountains calls for the melodies of Aaron Copland, so does a drive across a desert require the music of Pink Floyd. And so I hooked up Donna Mae's iTunes gizmo to a speaker dock, demanded quiet in the cab, and cranked up *Shine On You Crazy Diamond*, the haunting tribute to Sid Barrett, author of the group's psychedelic underpinnings, who lost his mind in the process, disappeared, and never shared in their worldwide acclaim. I tried to lose my own mind in my own world for a few luxurious minutes as the seductive music carried me past the simmering sand dunes.

But not everyone shared this cerebral commune – in fact, no one shared it – and I was obliged on several occasions to reiterate my call for quiet, wherein I received only begrudging acknowledgment. But I was relentless and ignored the philistines.

When the last note died, Donna Mae said, "Happy now?" and snatched the whole iTunes contraption from my grasp like I was a kid playing with razor blades. But I'm an easy going guy, and I was content. Half a loaf is better than no loaf at all.

With my one indulgence behind us, we returned our attention to gaining the famous Sosussvlei. There are other vleis in the area, smaller ones, called Hiddenvlei, !Naravlei, and Deadvlei, but Sousussvlei is the main attraction and therefore the namesake of the general area.

In years of extraordinary rains, the Tsauchab River, which empties into the Park from the mountains we had crossed the day before, has been known to carve its way through the sand and flow all the way to Sosussvlei, filling the pan with water. Ducks and flamingos wading in shallow pools amongst red sand dunes are said to be a surreal sight. That was hard to imagine in crackling heat so hot you could poach an egg in the palm of your hand.

This was one such blistering day, so it didn't seem like a good idea to go scouting around for minor vleis, especially one called *Deadvlei*. We voted to go straight to Sosussvlei and assess the next move from there.

Locating Sosussvlei is fairly simple. It is at the very *end of the road*, marked by a car-park that is accessible *only* by 4x4 vehicles. Now here are the statistics I spoke about earlier. The paved road ends at the 60 kilometer point – 5K short of the 4x4 car-park – and the track beyond is a sea of billowing sand masquerading as a road. There is an intermediate car-park at this 60 kilometer point, where 2x4 cars must park and their passengers wishing to find Sosussvlei must alight and hike the additional 5K to the 4x4 car-park.

It seemed redundant to me to park at the 2x4 car-park and hike 5K just to get to a point from which you have to hike back. What's 4x4 for, anyway?

It seemed redundant to John too. He stopped at the 2x4 car-park and engaged the four wheels in their lowest gear ratio.

"Hang on," he said, goosing the gas. He knows from his years in Africa not to address a 4x4 situation tentatively.

And he did not.

We hit the sand smartly, wheels spinning, sand flying. The Nissan bounced, bucked, lurched, and fish-tailed.

Each time I thought we were irretrievably mired in a fathom of sand, the car would leap free, as if of its own accord.

John plunged ahead, squeezing the steering wheel with the death-grip of a rodeo cowboy on a Brahma bull.

We continued in that fashion for 5 kilometers.

Finally we jounced onto solid gravel at the 4x4 car-park and my sphincter un-puckered.

Sossusvlei.

John parked under a scraggly camelthorn tree to savor the sparse shade and we settled into our established routine with a picnic lunch and a bottle of South African sauvignon blanc.

A couple of vervet monkeys sidled over looking for scraps and I threw out a crust. Someone yelled at me and they scattered. They were so cute; how could I not?

It's hard to hang out in the Namib Desert in 120 degrees, even in the shade, so we decided against looking for Deadvlei, or any other vlei for that matter. Instead, we took some photos by the decrepit Sosussvlei sign, hopped into the Nissan, cranked up the air-conditioning, and headed back to civilization via a circuitous route over some small sand dunes.

As John made to accelerate up the first dune, a woman appeared at the top jumping up and down, gesturing frantically for him to stop, which he did, leaving us stuck in the sand. The woman was trying to help her boyfriend who was sitting in his Toyota 4x4 several feet behind her stuck in the sand on the down-slope side of the same dune, directly in our path. He had been there for a half hour trying to get unstuck. Apparently this was not the best route to depart the area.

So we all piled out of the Nissan in the 120 degrees to make introductions and figure things out. Turns out the woman, Sandra, and her boyfriend, Tom, both Americans, are prominent members of the ex-patriot, public health community in South Africa, as are Melinda and John. They all knew each other by reputation but had never met. Peachy! It was 120 freaking degrees and we were having old home week.

Then along came a park ranger in a big, ten-passenger Land Rover without any passengers in it. He drove up the slight incline behind our Nissan to see what kind of trouble the stupid white folks had gotten themselves into and hopped out of his truck. Smirking faintly, he sauntered over and beheld the six of us – each with an advanced college degree, mind you – standing there in the hot blazing sun with our heads up our asses trying to figure out what to do next. He shook his head and got back in the truck and tried to back down the incline to get back on firmer ground from where he could pull us out. He wasn't so smart; his tires settled into the sand and he got stuck too.

By now John was rummaging about in the back of the Nissan, breaking out a giant canvas duffle-bag bulging with his secret weapons: a 30-foot nylon tow-rope with steel U-bolts on each end, and a pair of 15-foot-long metal treads like those of a battle tank. Back at the house, John had insisted on schlepping this stuff with us on the airplane and at the time I thought he was nuts. Upon seeing how proudly he presented these instruments – as if he had portended our need of them – I was convinced he was nuts. Don't get me wrong; this is the kind of guy to travel with in the African bush. But that's just me.

The park ranger took charge. He showed us how to rock his truck from side to side such that each up-stroke lifted the tires just enough to allow a small amount of sand to fall beneath them. After several bouts of such rocking, he explained, the tires on both sides would be worked up out of the sand. So we all rocked, it worked, he got free and backed down the incline onto firmer ground.

The things you learn in the desert.

Then we set John's treads down in the sand behind the rear tires of our Nissan and the ranger hooked the tow-rope up to his truck and pulled it out over the treads and down the incline.

Next we put the treads in front of Tom's Toyota and he was able to muscle it up over them and out of trouble.

Then we were all unstuck, whooping and hollering and high-fiving like we just discovered the tomb of Tutankhamen. We were also a little daft from dehydration after 45 minutes of cardio-vascular exercise in 120 degrees of shade-less desert sun. Of course, I may be exaggerating; maybe it was only 115 degrees.

At this point, the kindly park ranger didn't know what to do. I think we were scaring him. So we tipped him generously and he split.

Home free?

Not so quick.

John got the Nissan back to the 4x4 car-park where the clutch – apparently worn out from the strain of repeated attempts to get unstuck from the sand – promptly died. Tom and Sandra were behind us in the Toyota and saw our plight. John asked Tom to tow us out with the tow-rope and Tom agreed. He pulled us for about 2 kilometers until the Nissan sank into the sand so deeply that the nothing could budge it. Tom would risk blowing out his own clutch if he tried to pull us out, so that plan was dead.

That put us 63 kilometers from the *Sosussvlei Lodge* with a broke-down, stuck-in-the-sand, 4x4 Nissan that we now have to abandon. And it was still 120 degrees...or 115.

Our new friends, Tom and Sandra, turned out to be true friends. Or maybe they had no choice because they didn't want four dead, dehydrated bodies to be found slumped in the sand in the morning and linked to them by the park ranger. So they packed the four of us into the back seat of Tom's Toyota and hauled us back to the lodge.

There was a lot of thanking and hugging and us begging them to stay for sundowners. They were staying that night at the campsite at Solitaire and still had quite a ways to go before dark. The road between Sosussvlei and Solitaire, remember, is a most devilish dirt track, so they were understandably reluctant to tackle it in the dark with a buzz on. Wisely, they stayed for only one drink and in fifteen minutes were on their way. The four of us were still reeling from nearly spending the night in the Namib Desert under the watchful eye of the Southern Cross so we had us a few more pops to calm our nerves.

Now what?

An hour or so later, sufficiently mellowed, John called the car-hire company in Windhoek to discuss the predicament. In what I warrant was nothing less than an astounding, world-class negotiation, John convinced them to send out a replacement vehicle on a flatbed truck and then use it to haul back the broke-down Nissan 4x4 SUV which he had abandoned, sunk in the sand, 63 kilometers inside the Namib-Naukluft Park. I was amazed. Maybe John's power of persuasion was not the determining factor and the car-hire company was just used to this sort of thing. Who knows? In any event, they were sending out a truck with a replacement car in the morning, notwithstanding the five-hour drive from Windhoek to Sosussvlei, half of it over gravel track. Wow! That's a care-hire company.

The next morning we checked out of our rooms before 10:00, as was required, and hung around in the reception area with our luggage like refugees. At noon, John finally reached the car-hire office on his cell-phone and confirmed that the flatbed truck and replacement car had just left.

Around 4:00 PM, I got restless watching soccer games on television in the small air-conditioned conference room the lodge used to sequester lingering guests so I left the lodge and followed the hotel-workers' footpath across the bush and through a hole in an electrified fence to Sesriem.

The walk took less than twenty minutes but in a cloudless sky and 120 degrees, one gets thirsty.

I bought two cold beers in the tiny market – assuming I needed at least two to avoid succumbing to dehydration – and sauntered out into the dusty yard in front of the market building to drink them. In the middle of the yard, a lone skeletal tree cast filaments of shade on an unoccupied, straight-backed chair.

A tiny man was sitting in the sand between the tree and the chair, minding his own business. I hadn't noticed him before. One doesn't see everything perfectly in the Namib when the temperature is 120 degrees and blasts of shimmering heat-waves are billowing into the sky from the desert floor as if the very earth is on fire.

I sat down in the straight-backed chair.

Something didn't feel right.

I regarded myself holding two bottles of beer and the man none.

He was so close I could reach out and touch him, yet he didn't look over at me or otherwise acknowledge my presence.

But I could feel his thoughts: *Guy has two bottles of beer and I have none. Boy it's hot today.*

I felt stupid.

The picture seemed so absurd.

It was absurd.

I handed the man one of the beers.

He reached out slowly and took it, without registering a look of surprise, then nodded the faintest of gestures I took for a thank you.

He wore a bright blue, long-sleeve work shirt over shiny, long CalTrans-orange pants with holes in each knee big enough to reach through and tie his shoes. His choice of attire seemed somewhat unsuitable for lounging in the blistering Namib sun, but it did make sense for sitting in the dirt. It was apparent he did not have access to the fashions of the day and wore what he could get his hands on.

The man was rail-thin, almost to the point of emaciation, but he did not appear unhealthy. He had a kind face, although it was burnt to a very dark brown by the relentless sun, and when he raised the bottle to his lips I could see he lacked a few teeth. But his eyes were bright nonetheless.

After we had each taken a pull, I extended my right hand and introduced myself.

With a quickness that surprised me, he jumped to his feet to address me in a respectful fashion. He was about 5'6" and proffered his hand in the limp way that white folks are unaccustomed to. "My name is Simon," he said. "I'm the night watchman of the Park Gate."

Shaking his hand, I stood and asked, "You can have a beer?"

"It's okay; I don't go on duty for several more hours."

The ice broken, he commenced to tell me the part of his life story that mattered only on this particular day at this particular time, and mattered only to him. That is until he finished it.

He said he was 36 years old, the eldest son of four brothers. His father had died two weeks ago. He used this job to earn money to send back to his mother and three younger brothers so they could work their small farm in Mariental and feed themself. He hoped someday to buy animals, pigs and goats, to breed them, and to sell the offspring and improve the lot of the household for which he was now the head. He worked 24-day stretches, with 6 days off to go home and help out on the farm. His regular pay was the equivalent of US$70 a month, and he could earn another $15 by working extra days, but that left less time to help at home. He wasn't complaining, just telling his story.

Maybe he had embellished it, maybe he was conning me, but I didn't think so. It was clear he hadn't been sitting there in the hot sun fishing for tourists. And he sure wasn't blowing money on fashion and dental care.

I asked for his contact info and he ran into the market to get something to write it down. A minute later he emerged with his name and post office address scrawled in surprisingly neat capital letters on a small piece of cardboard. I gave him some money and said I would be in touch. I told him that since I didn't have a son and he didn't have a father that I hereby adopted him. He smiled at that, both of us not knowing what it really meant, or would lead to. But by then I had already decided it would lead to something. Stay tuned, I'm working on it.

We shook hands and said goodbye and I thought long and hard on the subject as I walked back through the hole in the fence to the lodge's parking lot where John was watching a flatbed truck unloading our replacement vehicle, a small 2x4 VW Golf.

John signed some papers taking possession of the replacement vehicle, and explained to the driver where he should find the Nissan, if it was still there. The driver was happy to go retrieve it by himself, which I couldn't understand, because I saw no winch on the flatbed truck. Was he going to levitate it? Maybe he did, because when we returned the VW in Windhoek the next day, the Nissan was sitting there in the car-hire yard. It remains his secret.

By the time we finally left the *Sosussvlei Lodge* it was a few minutes before 6:00 PM. We were anxious to get over the mountains on the gravel track to our overnight stop in Mariental before dark. There was no way to estimate the driving time in that terrain.

The mountains were an endless, ruptured landscape of rock outcroppings, rolling hills, and vast fields of grasses, green at the higher altitudes. We had plenty of time for casual conversation and I had a question to ask.

During the last two days at Sosussvlei, I had noticed John working his cell phone incessantly as if he were attending to some crises at his workplace. It was apparent from his phone demeanor that the calls were a matter of some importance and not mere chit-chat. I had reserved comment and minded my own business while my curiosity grew. By the time we left Sossusvlei and were bouncing along in the little VW Golf, it seemed that the matter had been put to rest. John and I had become quite good friends in the years since we climbed Kilimanjaro together and I felt that we knew each other well enough that I could ask him about it. I didn't want to put him on the spot with a direct question, so I tried to be oblique.

"I hope that business on the cell phone hasn't dampened your holiday," I ventured, leaning forward from the back seat.

"No, actually it has cheered me up," he said, in a tone that suggested he was glad I asked.

"Do tell," I said, feeling the door was open.

So he did.

"I've been arranging for Cedric, and his wife, Ntamsile, to stay at our house this weekend," John said casually. "Cedric is the headmaster at *Enjabulweni*, the orphanage in Swaziland where we adopted two of our kids so many years ago. Cedric and Ntamsile have driven up to Pretoria from Swaziland with their son, Menzi, to take him for treatment at hospital. He has what is called Factor 9 Deficiency, perhaps better known as Hemophilia B, the second most common type of hemophilia. Menzi is their last surviving son. He's only 8 years old. They've already lost two to AIDS and are paranoid about anything happening to Menzi. They watch him like a hawk because any little bump or bruise that would be commonplace in a young kid could be death to him. The calls were to arrange for them to have access to the house."

"Whew!" I said, flopping back in the seat and letting out a breath. "I guess I wasn't expecting a life or death issue."

"It's Mother Africa, my friend," John said. "That's what Africa is all about."

Approaching Mariental three hours later, just as it was getting full dark, the road became paved again. Melinda had booked us into an old guest-farm that advertised only six units so we weren't sure if we would be able to get anything to eat there upon our arrival, probably sometime after 8:00 PM.

We found the place down a long gravel driveway and pulled up to a reception area dominated by an open-air restaurant lit by a thousand lights. There were cars and busses in the parking lot and I thought surely we were in the wrong place. The restaurant was in full swing, serving full-course dinners to a boatload of guests. And a perky maitre d' welcomed us like long-lost relatives. We were floored.

Apparently the description of the place Melinda had read on-line was out of date. The farm had been purchased by a hospitality corporation, totally refurbished at considerable expense, and turned into a four-star resort. In its new incarnation, it had 46 rooms, a restaurant, bar, curio shop, and two swimming pools. We were cool with that.

So we had us a fine dinner after all, in the open-air restaurant beneath another clear and perfect starry sky. The

Southern Cross loomed high above as usual, inanimate guardian, incorruptible friend.

The next day we drove back to Windhoek to meet MaryBeth, the world's greatest schoolteacher.

We got a late start, leaving Mariental about noon. I hoped to arrive in time to pay a social visit to a lady friend of Joe Oakes. On learning that I was going to Namibia, Joe had suggested that an old beer-drinking buddy, MaryBeth, who was living there, was worth meeting. Joe is the Swim Director of the *Escape from Alcatraz Triathlon* and the world's greatest swimmer (*Bering Strait*). He is the kind of chap whose advice you can bank on. I had learned that first-hand.

Joe said MaryBeth was a gracious forty-something American, volunteer primary school teacher living in Windhoek. She teaches poor kids who otherwise would have no access to education at all. She is a volunteer in the purest sense of the word; she has no salary and earns no pay. She is associated with the mission of the MaryKnoll Fathers in New York and is supported entirely by them and by donations from friends and family. She has the exuberance of a teen-ager, the dedication of Mother Teresa, the tenacity of a bulldog, and a heart of gold. And she's a very nice person.

I had explained all this to my travelling companions and it was unanimous that we should try to meet her.

So now I called MaryBeth from the road to say we were just leaving Mariental and to express my concern that we might arrive too late in the day to meet her. It was the first time I had spoken to her. Without hesitation, she had said, "No problem. I'm house-sitting a fabulous mansion in Klein Windhoek, do you know where that is? Well you better find it because a party is underway here. I've got the two best Indian chefs in Namibia right here working the braai (African for barbecue). Just get your asses here as quickly as possible."

"Th-there's four of us," I stammered, caught a little by surprise.

"More the merrier," she said exuberantly. And we'd never even met her.

I was in hog heaven. With Indian food, I'm like a mad dog in a meat-house. The others thought it was a charming idea as well, so we went.

And MaryBeth welcomed four strangers like long-lost cousins.

The party had been going on for some time and the guests were well into the sauce. The center of attention was a large refrigerator bursting with spirits and mixers to which we were encouraged to enjoy an unfettered familiarity. So of course we did.

There were few guests: a pudgy effeminate chap from Dartmouth holding forth congenially on various political issues, a pretty German girl with a smile permanently affixed on her face as if she'd been into controlled substances (which she hadn't), a well-dressed Namibian girl who kept thanking the Lord and invoking the blessings of Jesus, and two sweaty Indian guys chained to the grill in the backyard patio. All of these folks were genuinely gracious and delighted to see the party enlarged.

The food was spectacular: curries, samosas, naan bread, raita. Cuisine of the gods.

Once freed from the grill, the Indian guys joined in animated conversation. They had been too busy to indulge in the spirits and had therefore maintained their ability to form a sentence. The other guests were no less convivial, just a tad more festive and a corresponding tad less articulate.

The next morning MaryBeth came to our B&B to say goodbye. She was carrying a book she had self-published and a plastic bag full of dolls.

"The book," she said proudly, "is entitled, *It Costs Almost Nothing – Beneficial Indoor Games and Handicrafts from Rubbish and Recycled Materials.* It's a primer for making games and toys out of nothing, a primer for my Namibian kids who have nothing."

Amazing! That's what she teaches. For free.

"The bag," she continued, "is full of exquisitely crafted, cloth dolls, hand-made by a Namibian lady who is trying to sell them to support her family and is having difficulty doing so because the local craft markets somehow prevent her from competing with them. I try to get ten bucks apiece for them, all of which goes to the lady, of course."

The dolls were indeed exquisitely crafted. There were ten in the bag. We bought all of them.

We had expected to say a simple goodbye to MaryBeth, instead we had our hearts jerked a bit. But it couldn't have turned out better. The dolls were perfect for the kids we would be visiting at the orphanages in Swaziland.

Then we hugged and took photos, thanked MaryBeth a hundredth time, and went to the airport.

5

Zimbabwe – 3 days, tour package, fully-catered

Back in Pretoria, we had a day at the Wilson house to wash clothes and re-pack for a side trip to Zimbabwe and Botswana I had booked for Donna Mae and me through *Rhino Africa Safaris*, a South Africa company headquartered in Cape Town. Aware that Zimbabwe was in political turmoil courtesy of its crooked president, Robert Mugabe, I had spoken by phone to the booking agent to discuss whether it was safe to go there. She assured me that business was being conducted as usual and that it was indeed safe.

John Wilson was not so optimistic.

I didn't want to come all this way and be denied the magnificent Victoria Falls, one of the great wonders of the world, because of a tin-horn dictator. I figured the more stars the package has, the safer it was likely to be.

The booking agent suggested a *five*-star package, three nights at the *Victoria Falls Safari Lodge* in Zimbabwe and two nights at the *Chobe Game Lodge* in

Botswana, all-inclusive, RT airfare Jo'burg-Vic Falls, airport transfers, in-country transport, fully-catered, game drives and river cruises. It was available at a great price. Cheaper than staying home.

I consulted the Oracle and she allowed we might give it a try.

So I booked it.

I have my own theory on this subject. I believe a five-star package of luxury accommodations is a treat as important to an overall Africa safari experience as the roll-your-own variety. It can get expensive but it's important to splurge for at least one. Airport and lodge transfers are painless, leaving your mind free to relax and savor the experience. Typically, airport transfers and longer drives are in air-conditioned vans, whereas short transfers are usually in open game-drive vehicles. Drivers are always friendly, reasonably articulate, and usually eager to chat. Lodges are normally located several miles into the bush and accessed by gravel roads, so trips in and out are very often game-drives in themselves.

This brings me to a discussion of the *open* game-drive vehicle versus the *closed* one. It is a slight tangent from our story but it is worth the diversion.

The *open* vehicle is like a convertible car: it has no hard top and no side windows. It is the standard for game-drives throughout *southern* Africa, where parks and game reserves are fenced and vehicular travel is restricted primarily to designated roads and tracks. This is not the case in Kenya and Tanzania where there are few fences, mostly vast open ranges where the wildlife flourishes unaided and migrates naturally. There, game-drives are usually conducted in *closed* vehicles, the trade-off being that the vehicles are *not* restricted necessarily to established tracks and can go anywhere across the plains in search of wildlife. I guess the theory for open vehicles in southern African countries is that since game-drives there are restricted to established tracks, there is better control of wildlife and therefore less risk of a critter jumping into your lap. Tell yourself that next time you're on a game-drive in an open vehicle and the driver pulls off-road and stops next to a lion that makes eye contact with you.

But even in a closed vehicle there is no guarantee of security if it has a pop-top, unless of course the top is closed. This point was emphasized to me on my first safari with Donna Mae some years ago. I had some bucks in those days so I had arranged private safaris with driver-guides for both Kenya and Tanzania. The vehicles in each country were 4x4 Toyota Land Rovers with a pop-top.

In the Ngorogoro Crater of Tanzania, we were cruising with the top open, marveling at the thousands of pink flamingos when we came upon a lion couple fornicating in broad daylight as if they were a lounge act. The way it works with lions is this: the male mounts the female from behind, takes four or five frantic pumps in the tempo of a jackhammer, then they both fall over and nap for fifteen minutes or so before repeating the exercise. This can go on for days. The lions have no shame and don't care if you park right next to them, which our driver did.

We watched this spectacle with unrestrained glee, cheering for the male lion as if it were an athletic contest. After one particularly energetic hump, the male flopped down to nap against our rear tire.

"We'll close the top now," the driver said quietly. "If I start the engine first or otherwise disturb him he will become very angry and quite unpredictable."

So somewhat after the fact, the top was secured and we waited an hour or so for the lion to flop down elsewhere so we could continue our safari.

The next day, still in Tanzania, we went on an open-top game-drive in Tarangire National Park looking for leopards lounging on tree branches. According to the guidebooks, it is the park's specialty. That may seem a stupid thing to do, but the driver assured us he knew the trees the leopards preferred and would not drive under one. We were not finding any leopards so the driver suggested a break and parked next to a large, leopard-less tree with overhanging branches.

"See that thin green branch laying on that fat one?" he said, pointing at a thick horizontal branch six or seven feet above the hood of our vehicle.

"The thin green one looks like it fell from above?" I said.

"Green mamba," he said with a straight face.

"Yikes!"

So much for security. In Africa, you take your chances.

The incident amused the driver and seemed to get him on a roll. He asked to tell a story about a friend who ran a gift shop. I liked the little trick with the green mamba so I said okay.

"My friend, he was driver like me," he began. "One day he was taking a Germany couple on a game-drive right here in Tarangire. They were also looking for leopard. They came upon one, sure enough, but it was fighting with a lion over some prey one of them had killed. My friend, he want to stay away, but the Germany guy, he say to get closer so he can stand up through the open top and take photos. We always do what the tourist want, so my friend, he drive closer. They are going round and round, the leopard and lion, but the lion, he scared, he want to get away from the leopard so he jump up onto the vehicle and into it through the top. The leopard, he chase after him, also right through the top and into the vehicle. They fight inside, but only each other, round and round, then jump out and go away. The Germany couple and my friend, they get little bit scratched up, but that is all. My friend, he now runs a gift shop."

I love this story. Even if they teach it at safari-drivers ed.

Our arrival at the Victoria Falls Airport was underwhelming. The place was small, untended and oddly claustrophobic. Customs and immigration officials were mechanically polite, bordering on sullen. Souvenir shops were few, and to say the goods on their shelves were unremarkable is being kind. Fortunately, a driver was waiting for us and we left the place so fast we didn't have time to dwell on its condition...or the reason behind it.

A van took us to the *Victoria Falls Safari Lodge*, located four kilometers outside of the small town of Victoria Falls on a west-facing plateau in its own private secluded bush. The lodge consisted of 72 newly-refurbished, ensuite rooms divided into two wings jutting out V-shape from a dramatic three-story, open-beam, central reception area, restaurant and bar. All structures were eco-friendly, made of dark rough-hewn timbers with thatched roofs, and overlooked a waterhole visited variously by springbok, kudu, elephant, warthog and guinea fowl.

We checked into our room and had a drink on the balcony watching a family of warthogs scuttling beneath a dead tree full of giant vultures. The warthogs dashed in a line like a high-speed commuter train, apparently heading straight for the waterhole.

The vultures weren't circling overhead so there wasn't anything dead in the vicinity yet.

A small herd of steenbuck poked at the ground on the sandy shore of the waterhole but none of them took a drink. I found that odd because the sun was high in a cloudless sky and the air was dry and hot. Shouldn't they be thirsty, I wondered? Must be a croc there.

Then a vervet monkey snuck in through the balcony door looking for something to steal.

"Get out!" Donna Mae shrieked, shattering the stillness of our wing of the hotel.

I spilled my drink.

The monkey back-flipped into the air and leaped off the balcony.

Donna Mae laughed at us.

The lodge had a shuttle that went to and from the town of Vic Falls on the half-hour, so we hopped on it. The driver was an affable chap and energetically pointed out the shops and hotels he thought would be of interest to us. Few were.

It was late in the afternoon so we elected not to get out of the bus and walk around. The driver took that as an opportunity to conduct a more elaborate round trip.

The town centre was small, dusty, and sparsely populated. It had a post office, bank, Spar Market, and a handful of tourist shops containing nothing new or exciting. Tucked in the back, just off the main thoroughfare, was a gigantic crafts market with rows of covered stalls bursting with bowls, wood carvings, fabrics, safari duds, and large Shona stone sculptures suitable for a village green.

A few years ago, Melinda bought an exquisite four-foot tall, one-hundred pound, Shona sculpture of an African woman from this very market. She had it shipped to Pretoria and it now stands majestically in the hallway of their house.

There were three hotels in the town centre: the *Ilala Lodge*, *Victoria Falls Hotel*, and the *Kingdom Hotel*.

The *Ilala Lodge* is a cozy, four-star hotel with 32 rooms decorated tastefully in British motifs and furnishings described in advertisements as evoking a bygone era (read colonial). The grounds and wide lawns are framed by the spray of the falls in the background.

The *Victoria Falls Hotel* is a five-star masterpiece, built in 1904. Known for its impeccable service, its colonial architecture and Edwardian-style furnishings, it is the best hotel in all of Zimbabwe. The grounds are immaculately kept and there is a private path to the falls. High tea is served there and the dining hall requires a jacket; two reasons I was glad we were staying in the bush.

The *Kingdom Hotel* is a 294-room, two-star monstrosity, built in 1999 at a cost of US$26.3 million. The architecture is faux-African, inspired by Great Zimbabwe, the famous archaeological ruins in Masvingo. The hotel was intended by President Robert Mugabe to be a national treasure and rekindle tourism in Victoria Falls, but it has come off garish and crude. There is a large food court with precious little food in it, and a sparkling casino where scant winnings are paid in the Zimbabwe dollars nobody wants. Mugabe has so trashed the country's economy – not to mention its international reputation – that foreign tourists are staying away from the place in droves. In fact, it seemed all of Victoria Falls was suffering a tourist drought, not just this sorry-ass hotel.

We were the only ones on the bus and the driver was in a chatty mood so I asked him, "What's with the scores of political posters we see on all the walls and posts demanding change?"

"Election Day is two days hence," he said, barely disguising his passion. I had opened a floodgate. Without missing a beat, he continued. "Most of the posters you see are for *MDC,* the main opposition party, called the Movement for Democratic Change. The face on those posters is the *MDC* candidate for president, Morgan Tsvangirai."

"Could you say that name again, please," I asked politely.

"Sang-gear-rye," he said slowly. When he saw I got it, he went on. "The fewer posters are those of the incumbent, President Mugabe. His party, *ZANU-PF*, dominates politics here and has been assuring his autocratic rule ever since our liberation from Britain in 1980 when Rhodesia became Zimbabwe. It is a shame. He was a great liberator, respected for that throughout Africa, but he has become a vile president. Everybody I know is hoping and praying that Morgan Tsvangirai will unseat him. It is time for change and important to spread that word."

In the short time we had been there, it looked to me that if change was needed anywhere, it was in Zimbabwe.

The tourist sees it straightaway. If you missed it at the airport, it's waiting for you right there in Victoria Falls, the tarnished crown jewel of Zimbabwe's tourist industry. A raging hyper-inflation – then at 231 million percent – was rendering the Zimbabwe dollar worthless. As a consequence, foreigners were required to make all payments and purchases *exclusively* with foreign currency.

That suited us fine but it was killing the local folks.

We saw a bizarre illustration of the impact the inflation was having on a local couple just finishing dinner at the *Victoria Falls Hotel*. They paid their restaurant tab with a two-inch-thick wad of Zimbabwe dollars the size of license plates.

Local folks didn't need a wallet to hold their money, they needed a wheelbarrow. Monopoly money was worth more than Zimbabwe dollars.

"That name, Tsvangirai," I said to the driver, "sounds familiar. Where have I heard it before?"

"Probably on BBC or CNN," he replied. "In 2002, he ran against Mugabe in the presidential election. It was surely rigged and Mugabe won. Then in 2004 he was acquitted of treason in a trial alleging a plot to assassinate Mugabe. And just last year, he was arrested and beaten in custody by government officials. His bloody face was on the world news."

"Yes, yes," I said. "I remember seeing that."

"I wish more people had," he said sadly.

The political situation here was shameful. Tragic. What had we blundered into?

I needed to learn more.

The next day, I sought out shopkeepers, hotel clerks, ordinary citizens, anyone who would chat with me. And most everyone did.

Donna Mae (J.D. with a B.A. in Political Science) was as curious as I. But she was hesitant about bluntly questioning locals on sensitive political matters. She kept unusually quiet (dare I say, *blissfully* quiet). I was being the loudmouth tourist so she let me break the ice and ask the difficult questions. She hung on every answer though.

Universal opinion seemed to be that the absurd hyper-inflation was caused solely by one man: Gideon Gono, the Governor of the Reserve Bank of Zimbabwe (the RBZ). Apparently, his fiscal solution was to keep printing money in ever increasing denominations.

"But Gono is not the root cause of our plight," one shopkeeper said, contemptuously. "That honor goes to His Excellency, Robert Gabriel Mugabe. He is an 84-year-old tyrant. He has ruled continuously for 28 years since the liberation. He has ruined us. It is time for him to go."

In town the next day, I talked to an emaciated young man hawking key chains and small African carvings. He fairly spit out his disgust: "Mugabe is intelligent, charismatic, corrupt, ruthless, and untrustworthy. Otherwise, he's a nice guy."

The more I talked to the people, the more I learned. And the worse it got.

Mugabe had showed his hand right from the start. In 1982, he entered into an agreement with Kim Il Sung for North Korean soldiers to train a special brigade, called the

Fifth Brigade, that would operate at his command, outside of the national army structure. Where did he get that idea, I wonder? Schutzstaffel ring a bell?

That year, Mugabe faced a guerilla insurgency in Matabeleland, fomented by a small group of dissidents from a rival political party. The guerillas were a determined group that proved elusive and difficult to eliminate. It was their misfortune to be of the Ndebele tribe, historically hated by the Shona people whose god on earth was Robert Mugabe. Rather than taking the direct road and rooting the guerillas out militarily, Mugabe took a path of less resistance. In an operation known as Gukurahundi (Shona for floods or rains that wipe away rubbish), he allowed the Fifth Brigade to be unleashed upon the civilian population from which the guerillas were drawn. Some even say he personally ordered it.

Mugabe's detractors claim the Fifth Brigade slaughtered at least 20,000 Ndebele citizens over a period of five years, maybe even 30,000. Mugabe denies it. But a claim of that magnitude cannot be pure fantasy. Calls for a proper inquiry of the matter and a redress of grievances survive to this day.

It would seem Mugabe has earned a trip to The Hague for that atrocity alone.

Yet still he rules.

Where are the voices?

There's more: Mugabe's land redistribution scheme, commenced in late 1999. This brainstorm was designed to lead eventually to the wholesale takeover of all of the country's 4,000-plus, white-owned commercial farms, which to that point had earned Zimbabwe a reputation as the "breadbasket" of southern Africa.

It is a clear reflection of Mugabe's world-class hard-on for the White Man. Who can blame him? He was a political prisoner of Ian Smith's white-dominated Rhodesian regime for 10 years from 1964 to 1974. Some accounts claim that he earned as many as six college degrees during that period. But sadly, none of that education contributed a dollop of wisdom to a notion of reconciliation or a plan of nation building.

According to Mugabe's sales pitch, the farms were to be parceled out to landless blacks as redress for the wrongs of the country's colonial past. Instead, he awarded (and as of this writing is continuing to award) most of the farms to political cronies and loyalists within his ruling party, with no meaningful compensation to the ousted owners, and no plan to insure the farms' continued production by the new owners. At its worst, mobs attacked white farmers and families, beat them, killed some, threw them out, and burned and ransacked their homes. According to those I talked to, there were still a few hundred white-owned farms, and the farm invasions did not seem to be over.

For Mugabe, the land redistribution scheme has been a two-pronged opportunity. He grandstands his righting of the wrongs of colonialism *and* purchases a loyal power base with the spoils. For Zimbabwe, it has been a disaster. The government has not provided necessary resources – educational, material, or financial – to new black owners and as a consequence, most of the farms taken over have not returned to productivity. Agricultural production has nose-dived, setting off a chain reaction that has destroyed a once-thriving economy.

At our hotel, I talked to an articulate bartender who was a schoolteacher in an earlier life and could not make ends meet on the peanuts the government paid him. He lamented, "Shelves are empty in the shops, medicine is unavailable, jobs are scarce, unemployment exceeds 80%, and educated citizens are fleeing the country. Not to mention the hyper-inflation over 231 million percent is the highest in the world.

"Meanwhile, Mugabe continues to blame everything on sanctions imposed by the western powers, notably the U.S. and Britain. But the sanctions are financial and visa restrictions imposed on *individuals*, on Mugabe and certain of his cronies *personally*. They are not restrictions on the country. It is classic Mugabe misdirection.

"But nobody is fooled. Mugabe is the problem, short and simple. Gideon Gono, the inflation genius, is his appointed lackey and also his personal banker. Together, they make sure that loyalists are paid and that Mugabe maintains his lavish lifestyle, both at home and abroad. While we starve, he vacations at his mansion in Hong Kong where a daughter attends college and his wives shop with impunity.

"He has announced publicly he will rule Zimbabwe as long as he lives. He has been making good on that promise by election-rigging for more than a decade. At 84, he is still up to his old tricks, and there is no indication he will change. He is one leopard that will never change its spots. Zimbabwe will not be free until he dies or someone makes him dead."

"Yikes!" I exclaimed. "Subversive language that."

The bartender acknowledged my comment with a wry smile.

I looked around for government agents but it was a slow hour of the day and we were mercifully alone.

Later in the day, I found another shopkeeper happy to chat. It felt like I had tapped into a pattern where every citizen was eager to pick up a conversation where the last one left off.

"Perhaps we are being too harsh on Mugabe," he said. "After all, he has shown a big heart. Look how generously he has treated his old friend, Mengistu Haile Mariam, the former dictator of Ethiopia? In 1991 he welcomed Mengistu with open arms and ensconced him in luxurious quarters at government expense, where he sits today."

This shopkeeper was a kindly old gentleman, and he allowed he had his own reasons for harboring resentment on the subject of Mengistu but he would not belabor me with them. I listened attentively as he did so emotionally for the next half-hour. He threw out facts and figures at light speed and I could not remember a tenth of them. Back home I did my own research to refresh my memory.

The condensed version is that Mengistu came to power in Ethiopia brutally in 1977 when he emerged as the leader of the *Derg*, a military junta that had overthrown Emperor Haile Selassie three years earlier. Mengistu ruled Ethiopia with a bloody hand until 1991 when he fled to Zimbabwe. During his tenure, local government militias and security surveillance units had systematically murdered tens of thousands of "counterrevolutionaries" opposed to his policies, not the least of which was the transformation of Ethiopia's old feudo-capitalist economic system to a Marxist-Leninist one. Companies, private businesses, and land were nationalized without compensation in an aborted attempt to spread the wealth. Droughts and famines were a regular occurrence that should have been Mengistu's responsibility to mitigate, but he was too busy imposing his tyrannical rule upon the people to discharge that responsibility. The people suffered miserably.

Have some of Mengistu's strong-armed tactics rubbed off on Mugabe? Most likely. They go back a long way. Mengistu helped train Mugabe's liberation army. Since Mengistu has been in Zimbabwe, it has been reported that he has advised Mugabe on security and other such matters related to perpetuating Mugabe's hold on absolute power. Of course, those reports have been denied by the government, but the parallels are there for all to see.

The shopkeeper concluded his story with words I do remember: "Mengistu Haile Mariam flushed his country down the toilet just as Robert Gabriel Mugabe has done with Zimbabwe."

As an aside, our brothers in the Rastafarian community might take note that in 1975, Emperor Haile Selassie was assassinated, almost certainly by the *Derg*, if not by Mengistu Haile Mariam's own hand. *Haile Selassie* was the emperor's regnal name. He was born *Lij Tafari*, and later took the pre-regnal title *Ras*, thus becoming *Ras Tafari*.

Back at the *Safari Lodge* I went into the television lounge to check on news of the day.

A white Zimbabwean lady who was also a guest at the hotel was watching a local news story about the coming election and shaking her head. I asked her what she thought about it and she freely admitted to a perfect stranger that she dearly wished for Morgan Tsvangirai to win, but alas, she didn't expect it.

"I know Mugabe all too well," she said with a sigh. "He has rigged every other election and the likelihood he will rig this one – the one with the best chance of ending his reign, mind you – is a given. Naturally, I'll vote tomorrow anyway. The magnitude of opposition sentiment must be shown if the will of the people is ever to prevail."

She seemed to be in a chatty mood and I wished to hear something about white folks' life in Zimbabwe. I chanced to ask, "So how are you making your living?" and in so asking, opened another can of worms.

Without hesitation, she said, "Somehow we still own our farm. We grow and export flowers. The government encourages our business, probably, I guess, for its source of foreign currency."

"Foreign currency is that important to the government?" I asked naively.

"Oh yes. Since nobody on the planet will accept the Zimbabwe dollar, the government needs foreign currencies for its international financial transactions. To help with that problem, the Reserve Bank of Zimbabwe requires all businesses dealing with outsiders to maintain a Foreign Currency Account which they monitor and regulate at will. So the good news is we still have our farm; the bad news is the RBZ treats our Foreign Currency Account like it's their piggy bank, routinely and arbitrarily withdrawing funds from it."

"Jesus," I blurted. "Why don't you just leave?"

"I wouldn't think of it," she said proudly. "I was born and raised in Zimbabwe; it's my country and I won't abandon it…or be run out."

Ballsy lady! I admired her pluck.

Later that night, I had occasion to chat with an articulate young student concerned for the future of his people and passionately hoping for change. His exact words wring in my ears today: "If Tsvangirai wins, it is a new dawn for Zimbabwe. If Mugabe wins, the sun sets on us." A sad thought to sleep on.

In the morning, as if to wash away the melancholy of the night before, we struck out early for our guided tour of Victoria Falls. A van took us to a parking lot lined with craft stalls where a guide handed us rain slickers and said, "Follow me."

Victoria Falls is fed by the Zambezi River. The falls are 1700 meters across, making it the longest continuous curtain of falling water on earth. The average height of the falls is 92 meters. At full flood – when we were there – over 550 million litres of water cascade over the falls per minute. The volume of pounding water sends a spray plume 500 meters high.

The Zambezi River originates in the far northwest corner of Zambia. It flows south through Angola and returns to Zambia where it twists and winds and is fed by various tributaries. Eventually it comes alongside a small length of Namibia's Caprivi Strip, joins Botswana's Chobe River, and becomes the boundary between Zambia and Zimbabwe.

The best viewing of the falls is from the Zimbabwe side via a tourist trail that meanders along the top of the deep gorge parallel to the curtain of falling water. The gorge is the continuation of the Zambezi River. Looking across at the falls from the tourist trail, you are looking at Zambia. Viewing the falls from the Zambia side would be like watching a play from backstage.

The tourist trail commences opposite the falls' first cataract, aptly named *Devil's Cataract*, and proceeds easterly towards the famous iron bridge. The spray plume increases progressively as you go along the trail until you are in monsoon conditions, soaked through and fairly uncomfortable, rain slicker or not. Ceremoniously, I eschewed the rain slicker, preferring a royal communion with nature. Donna Mae did not.

The *Devil's Cataract* is the introduction to the awesome power of the falls. Its lookout point is the closest tourists can get to any part of the falls. It is the closest anyone of sound mind would want to get to the falls.

The lookout point was ringed by a flimsy railing that wobbled precariously within scant meters of unimaginable volumes of water thundering rapidly over the brink. The force of the pounding water was terrifying, the roar of it deafening, making it one of nature's most powerful natural acts. The lookout point is one of few places on earth where one can stand safely in proximity to a natural act of that magnitude.

Peering into the *Devils Cataract* is hypnotic, evoking a dreamlike sensation of being drawn, beckoned, down into the maelstrom and through the boiling gorge below. It is chicken-skin time, akin to leaning over the rim of Hawaii's Halemaumau Fire Pit, or standing before 30-foot breakers at Waimea Bay. Other examples of precarious proximity to immense natural power – earthquake, tornado, on-coming Rhino – are not experienced voluntarily, let alone safely, and are not quite the same.

Late that afternoon, a *Wild Horizons* van picked us up and took us and a bunch of other tourists to a small dock on the banks of the Zambezi River. There, we boarded a small flat-bottom boat for the sundown cruise.

The boat had a canvas shade roof, an outboard motor, six tables with chairs, platters of snacks, and a cooler full of drinks. A dozen or so tourists were arrayed about the tables with drinks in hand and cameras at the ready, the classic tourist experience. I was liking it.

I walked to the far railing of the boat and leaned out to feel the river's essence.

"Sit down, you're rocking the boat," snapped Donna Mae.

I sat.

The boat captain started the motor, cast off the ropes, and headed out into the river.

An Afrikaner guy lit up a cigarette and the boat captain said, "Sir, you cannot smoke unless everyone on the boat agrees it is okay. That's the rule."

The Afrikaner guy grumbled something unintelligible.

The boat captain said, "Does everybody agree it is okay?"

We all looked around at each other, somewhat uncomfortably, but nobody agreed.

The Afrikaner guy fumed.

It seemed incomprehensible. This jerk could not understand that on an immaculately clear day in the middle of the magnificent Zambezi River, the flow of it smooth, the smell of it unspoiled, nobody wanted to share his smoke.

The boat captain said, "Well, sir, then you must put out your cigarette."

"No!" the Afrikaner barked, throwing his cigarette in the river with a flourish. "Take me back to the shore."

The boat captain turned the boat around and took him back to the shore.

The Afrikaner stormed off the boat. His fat wife waddled meekly after him.

It was unclear if he was pissed off because he couldn't smoke, or because it was put to him by a black man. Clearly the latter irked him, so it was probably both.

Nobody said a word but every face on the boat had a look that read, "Asshole!"

The boat captain headed back out into the river and some light laughter ensued.

The sundown cruise now began in earnest.

The Zambezi was wide, more than a mile across to the opposite shore. Someone exclaimed, "Wow, that's a big river."

The boat captain said, "That's not the far shore you're looking at; that's just an island. The river goes around it and is just as wide on the other side."

Jesus! I'd seen mighty rivers before, the Hudson, Mississippi, Thames, Tiber, Danube, Nile; was the Zambezi the grand-daddy of them all? Today it was. *Love the one you're with.*

The river ignored these reminisces and continued flowing gustily towards the falls several miles downstream. Spray mist billowed ominously in the distance, a mile wide and high in the sky.

Tourist cruises ply the river every day of the year without mishap, but I couldn't stop myself from wondering what happens if our weeny little outboard motor fails. I didn't see a spare motor or an anchor. I supposed the boat captain had a walky-talky to call in emergencies. But what good would that do but send gawkers to the lookout at the *Devil's Cataract* to watch the flying boat.

I spent most of the cruise with one eye looking for the nearest shore.

But the boat captain knew his stuff. He took us upriver straightaway and pointed out a giant croc lying on the shore.

I thought that was good marketing: show the whiteys the croc first, that way they're happy and he can take his time finding the hippos. This he did, and soon found not one but two hippo pools full of the monsters. We clicked away at dozens of eyes, ears and noses and a couple of gaping yawns big enough to swallow a Volkswagen.

In truth, the cruise was most enjoyable, made even more so by the sounds of wildlife, the smell of Africa, the pulse of the Zambezi, the setting sun, and the romance of Safari.

Not to be overlooked: the cooler full of drinks, an essential component of a sundown cruise. A couple vodka martinis are not only so, so chic, but great to take your mind off looking for the nearest shore.

That night in the lodge's restaurant, we were entertained by an a cappella singing group called *Amazulu Cultural Ensemble*. The group was comprised of eight tall gentlemen who performed without the aid of any musical accompaniment, in the traditional southern African style known as *mbube*. Their sound, frugally employing click consonants, was sophisticated, melodic and peaceful, very similar to that popularized world-wide by the Grammy-winning South African group, *Ladysmith Black Mambazo* (check them out on YouTube, you will thank me).

Naturally I bought *Amazulu's* CD, and nothing could keep us from having dinner at the lodge again the next night to see them once more.

The next day I booked an elephant safari.

"What is that exactly?" asked Donna Mae skeptically.

"Outside of town there's an elephant conservation camp that conducts rides in the bush on the backs of elephants. There'll be a trained driver who drives the thing, and we just sit there behind him and try not to fall off. Pretty cool, huh?"

"Both of us sit behind him?"

"Yeah!"

"Isn't that a lot of people on one elephant?"

"It's a big elephant."

A *Wild Horizons* van picked us up at 3:00 PM and drove for about an hour into the bush over a rugged gravel road to the elephant place. In better times it was a popular game park, lodge, campsite, and elephant conservation camp. Now it was only the latter, a microcosm of the Zimbabwe tourist industry in general, decimated almost to extinction – along with every other crucial industry – by Robert Mugabe's guiding hand. What was left here was a struggling elephant conservation camp, making ends meet by offering elephant rides to tourists. But the facilities we saw, including the lodge's reception and dining area, had been maintained properly so there was no feeling of a tourist scam at a down-and-out operation. Quite the opposite, as it turned out.

There were four couples on the safari. We sat in camp chairs in the reception yard and the head elephant dude handed out glasses of punch and gave us a short briefing about the place and elephant lore in general.

"Almost all of the elephants we acquire are orphans," he began. "They have been rescued from some situation – injury, illness or abuse – that prevents them from living in the wild. They are cared for here, trained, and bred. Some of the off-spring will be released into the wild and some will be trained for these safaris."

"Why do elephants have one tusk shorter than the other?" somebody asked.

"That's from use," the elephant dude answered. "They use one of their tusks more often than the other, in the same fashion that humans are right-handed or left-handed."

"What about their teeth?" someone asked.

"Unlike humans, who get two sets of teeth, baby and adult, elephants get six. The new teeth grow in as the old ones wear down. When the last set wears out, the elephant can no longer masticate properly and usually dies of starvation or malnutrition."

I was so enjoying myself in the warm sun and the wild Zimbabwe bush that a smart-ass comment began to form on the tip of my tongue. I was furrowing my brow, working to refine it, when Donna Mae caught the look on my face and poked me in the ribs.

"Don't!" she whispered, in that gruff command-voice that comes naturally to wives like poking in the ribs.

I didn't.

The elephant dude asked if there were any more questions, and with me holding my tongue there were none, so he gave out a few rules for dealing with elephants and advised sternly that we should follow them.

He brought out four large elephants, assigned one to each couple, introduced us individually to our elephant – if you can picture that – and showed us how to approach and pet him. He gave each of us a handful of marble-size pellets for the elephant to take with his trunk from the palm of our hand. It sounded easy enough but it was a little disconcerting when the monster caught wind of a potential snack and his trunk flailed around like a rubber telephone pole inches from my face.

Then we were left alone for a few minutes to get acquainted. This made sense, although one feels a bit silly saying, "nice elephant, that's a good boy," to a four-ton pachyderm. It is quite surreal, but a good idea if you plan to get on its back.

I was a bit tentative at first, but when the four-ton monster looked me square in the eye, the elephant dude's rules jumped instantly to mind.

That caused me to reflect on a curiosity: the human male, the white one of the species, often believes he is Chosen and, therefore, is exempt from certain rules. This is not the case in Africa; the rules apply to everyone.

Example No. 1: You are on a game drive in an open vehicle. The driver stops within ten feet of a 400-pound lion minding its own business. You are seated next to the door on the lion-side of the vehicle. You lean out to get a good photo of the lion, whose attention you have just drawn. The driver says, "Don't lean out of the vehicle." No explanation is necessary. You see the point instantly and so you don't.

Example No. 2: At a rest stop, you encounter baboons. They are cute. Some of them are as big as you. You would love to offer them some morsels from your bag of chips. A ranger says, "They are not friendly. They have very sharp teeth. They will snatch food from your mouth and rip your lips off. Stay away from them." Same deal, so you do.

Example No. 3: You return from your elephant ride. You are rapturous from the experience. You climb down from the elephant and make to approach him with open arms, to hug and kiss him. The elephant dude says, "Don't do that; he is hungry now and won't take kindly to it." By now you've got the picture, and so you don't.

It's like that in Africa. No grey area in the bush. More things than skin are black & white.

So off we went in a tidy group, four elephants with three humans upon each, escorted by an armed guide on foot trailing a baby elephant, its handler, and a videographer.

The guide said his rifle was for firing a warning shot to disperse wild bull elephants that occasionally show up looking to make jiggy-jiggy with his female elephants. I was cool with the man's explanation, whether it was the real reason or not. Packing heat in the bush is never a bad thing.

There were few animals about: a dozen springbok, some warthogs, and a family of giraffe across the lake. The elephant's gait was ponderous and leisurely. It did not flow as one might expect, rather it heaved in no discernible cadence as the beast's mighty paws negotiated the irregular terrain. Nor were we in any hurry. How many elephants does one ride in a lifetime? Moreover, we had some time to talk politics with the driver straddling the elephant's neck in front of Donna Mae.

He was a handsome black man, educated and articulate, with a wife and a young daughter. He said his wife was working but he told her to stop because her pay was too meager and half the time her employer didn't pay her at all. When they get sick, they have to go to Botswana to get medicine. He was a knowledgeable and experienced animal handler, specializing in elephants, which placed him among the precious few in Zimbabwe able to find employment. He and his family would be fine as long as he stayed in the tourism industry, which he hoped would remain intact given the compelling beauty of Zimbabwe and its dependence on foreign currency.

The next day was our last in Zimbabwe. It was also Election Day. I had mixed emotions about leaving on the eve of a seminal event. Every living soul I had spoken to wanted Mugabe out and Tsvangirai in. But it seemed a sea-change was not inevitable and there was just a little tension in the air.

The gripping question was how Mugabe would prevail yet again: how he would cheat the people this time. Some that I talked to were enthusiastic about a new law that had been passed requiring election results to be posted at each polling place immediately after the polls closed. The new law was inspired so that the vote count would be posted for all to see, rendering a real-time result that could not be altered at a later date. Previously, all results were sent to a central location in the capital, Harare, where Mugabe and his *ZANU-PF* henchmen manipulated them at will. The new law was intended to preclude such abuse of the electoral process.

I was sad for these beautiful people who just wanted to live in peace, feed their families, and participate in free and fair elections. On top of the political repression, cronyism, and lawlessness, Mugabe had starved them half to death. They couldn't win for losing.

I tipped generously, trying to convince myself that rich tourists are important to their struggling economy. Are we? John had taught me how to palm the tip and slip it surreptitiously to the waiter to preclude it being confiscated by the employer on behalf of the government.

We can't do anything about their corrupt political system, but we can give our tips straight to the people. It's a small gesture but little things can add up. The way to eat an elephant is one bite at a time.

Whew! On to Botswana.

6

Botswana – 3 days, tour package, fully-catered

In the morning, another *Wild Horizons* van drove us west for about an hour to the border. Before stepping into Botswana, we had to get out of the van and walk through some kind of disinfectant gunk to kill Zimbabwe cooties.

"See any symbolism here?" I asked Donna Mae.

"Not a smidgen."

"Botswana is a stable democratic country," I began. "It is one of the few shining lights in Africa, the polar opposite of Zimbabwe. The president of Botswana, Ian Khama, is one of the few African leaders to speak out publicly against Mugabe for the destitution he has caused. Footprints from that destitution are not welcome to infect Botswana soil."

"Dig deep for that one, Einstein?"

"I don't do deep."

"Then get your passport out and keep your mouth shut if you want to get into Botswana."

"Yes, Memsahib."

The Botswana immigration and customs officials were pleasant and cheerful, unlike the Zim folks who weren't but probably would have been if they were not so hungry.

We schlepped our luggage across the border where a cheerful older gentleman wearing a name tag that said *Gray* muscled the bags into the back of an open van. Showing several teeth in a large mouth, he said, "Welcome to Botswana, folks. Hang on," and took off at Nascar speed.

The road was tarred – probably during the reign of Hadrian – and it seemed that the total area of the potholes exceeded the area of remaining tar. This was just my observation and proved to be of no consequence to our intrepid driver. He dodged the potholes in dizzying sweeps for half an hour until we finally arrived at the gate of the Chobe National Park with white knuckles and blue nausea. He signed us in and headed down a gravel road to the *Chobe Game Lodge*, the only permanent lodge inside the park.

The gravel road was smooth as a billiard table.

The driver raced down it at a dizzying four miles per hour.

Something seemed odd to me. I wondered why he would drive recklessly on a tarred road and slowly on a smooth one.

Almost instantly, as if conjured up to answer the question, the long necks of a family of giraffe appeared, gliding along above the thick vegetation some twenty yards to our right, matching our speed. Two skittish warthogs dashed across the road in front of us and a group of springbok antelopes darted off into the bushes.

A welcoming committee.

And a mini game drive.

Tourist literature says the *Chobe Game Lodge* was the site of the second wedding of Elizabeth Taylor and Richard Burton, but I didn't see any plaque to authenticate that. And I looked. The cheerful gentleman tending a small bar didn't even know what I was talking about when I asked him if it were true. "Elizabeth who?" he said politely. He was such a pleasant chap, however, that I ordered a martini and we discussed a wide range of subjects for an hour. He was right. He knew more about the decipherment of Linear B and the sequencing of the human genome than he did about Elizabeth Taylor.

Nevertheless, the *Chobe Game Lodge* was a most commodious place. Unlike the rustic architecture of the *Vic Falls Safari Lodge*, it was contemporary, graceful, smooth-walled stucco and concrete, muted colors, soft white leaning to grey. Flooring in the public areas was quarry tile throughout, light grey, easy on the eyes.

The lodge sat conveniently on the banks of the Chobe River that flows into the Zambezi and fit nicely with the soft tones of the river's shoreline. An open bar and dining area looked over a wide manicured lawn to the river. The place screamed five-star.

There were 46 rooms, each furnished lavishly with Rhodesian teak furniture and decorated with African carvings and accessories.

Our room was sumptuously appointed, and unnecessarily air-conditioned. The bed was draped with mosquito netting as is typical in luxury lodges whether in malaria areas or not. A large balcony looked down on a lawn being manicured by the house warthog and over the river at a herd of cape buffalo dallying far in the distance.

The room oozed sensuality.

Perfect for jiggy-jiggy.

Dinner at night was a braai, set up in the open down by the river. There were a dozen or so tables with candles, and a musical group with dueling xylophones.

Sizzling on the braai were springbok, kudu, warthog and crocodile. Donna Mae tried the springbok and kudu. I had the vegetables and lot of white wine.

It was a warm and sultry night, sounds of wildlife mingling with the almost imperceptible murmurs of the Chobe River, the kind of night you wish would never end. Were it not for the jarring tones of the two competing xylophones we might have lingered there for some time.

We returned to our room across the wide lawn – the warthog's lawn – continuing to luxuriate in the balmy exoticness of a Botswana night, both of us expressing an odd sensation, not of being followed, rather of being accompanied somehow. We looked up together, our eyes drawn automatically to the same spot in the sky, to the Southern Cross, our new friend.

There are many other constellations in the southern sky, but there are none so prominent, so regal, so insinuating, that its own magnetism draws your eye to it instantly and without uncertainty. The result is an intangible affection, similar to that which the Japanese have for Fuji-san and I have for Kilimanjaro.

In the morning we went out on the 6:00 AM open-vehicle game drive. We were the only ones this particular day. In regard to wildlife, it was a bust. Moreover, we hadn't dressed properly, we were uncomfortably cold, and we didn't even see a warthog. Some game drives are like that. It doesn't ruin your day, quite the opposite depending on what you compare it to. I thought about the choking rush-hour traffic on the I95 freeway in Connecticut, the 405/5 freeway merge in California, and the countless other of our new-wave freeway jams. Those thoughts were thoroughly depressing; how could I complain about this place? We were alone in a pristine wilderness, silent but for the chugging of the diesel engine and the scraping of scraggly foliage on the sides of our ride.

There was a beauty to this area of the park, so subtle it could easily be missed. The beauty was not so much as in what the place *was,* as in what it *was not.* There were no buildings, no signs, no street lights, no concrete, no neon, no jarring cacophony of civilization, no evidence of humans ever having been there save the dirt track upon which we bounced. There were no shimmering golden vistas as in the savanna of the Masai Mara or the blinding pink clouds as in the flamingos of the Ngorogoro Crater. No sir, not this landscape. Dull of palette, unspectacular in presentation, it was as soothing to its visitors as surely it must be to its own savage beasts.

The Bush.

But we still needed our animal hit, so in the afternoon we went on another game drive to a different area of the park. There were ten of us so the lodge brought out the largest vehicle in its fleet: a 4x4 open truck with the shock absorbers of a troop carrier. It was an ungainly machine with three rows of seats behind the driver, each row slightly higher than the one in front of it. The people in the top row get the best views but they also get seasick.

We sat right behind the driver.

Wildlife was everywhere, as if a gate had been opened at 4:00 PM and animals were let out as compensation for the meager morning.

Rather quickly, we came upon a large herd of elephants. There were dozens of them, grazing on a scraggly hillside, minding their own business.

Until we came along.

The driver pulled in amongst them and cut the engine. The herd bull, the largest of the group, was the size of a battle-tank. He stood ten yards diagonally to our front and shifted uneasily, fixing us with a menacing stare. Ears the size of garage doors flapped wildly.

"He's testing us," said the driver over his shoulder.

"You don't say?" I mumbled.

Donna Mae elbowed me in the ribs.

Here was one of the true anomalies of the safari experience: some drivers will creep up tentatively to a group of elephants and whisper for quiet and no quick movements, while others will charge in with reckless abandon, bellowing odd tidbits of pachyderm lore. Our driver preferred the latter approach, and thankfully (since we lived to tell about it) because it is just that unexpected element of real danger that contributes greatly to the completeness of the safari experience.

We were not attacked by the herd bull, although he never took his eyes off us. Eventually the driver moved on to annoy the lesser herds of springbok, troops of vervet monkeys, several rhino, and a family of giraffe.

The drive was slow and peaceful in the warm afternoon, and it too never wanted to end.

As the sun settled lower in the west and I expected the driver to take the next turn leading back to the lodge, he surprised me. He turned in his seat, and with the first genuine smile I had seen from him all day, he said over his shoulder, "Now for the lions."

Those among us who had started to doze off snapped awake.

He drove a short way along a track parallel to the Chobe River, swerving in and out of dense brush until finally entering into a gently sloping expanse of shoreline ringed by acacia trees. He stopped suddenly and cut the engine, smack dab amid three adult female lions lounging in the sand as if they were having a day at the beach.

Two lions were within 15 feet of the right side of the vehicle, and one lion was 20 feet off to the left side. These were no pussycats.

I guessed they must have eaten recently because they showed no interest in the truckload us...who were showing great interest in them.

There was a lot of fidgeting with cameras, some shifting in seats, and very hushed *oohs* and *aahs*. Sure enough, a guy started to lean out to take a photo. I saw it coming and nudged Donna Mae with my elbow, making the *watch-this* motion with my eyes.

I smirked and waited.

"Don't lean out of the vehicle," the driver said, in a hushed tone.

I barely managed to stifle a laugh.

"You're sick," Donna Mae murmured.

The next morning we were driven back to the border and transferred into another *Wild Horizons* van that took us back to the Victoria Falls Airport.

Departing Botswana was uneventful, departing Zimbabwe was not.

We had a long wait for our plane so we went into the airport lounge for a drink.

The lounge had a floor plan comprised of concentric circles, the inner-most of which was the bar, set on a raised platform, with bar stools affixed to the platform. The next concentric circle was an aisle at ground level. Farthest out, against a round white wall with glass-block inserts, was another raised platform with tables on it.

There was no attendant at the bar, nor were there any of the normal accoutrements suggesting the bar had been in use in this decade. All of the seats on the bar-stool posts had been ripped off except one that dangled to the floor, yet to be wrenched loose from its connections.

There were eight tables on the outer platform, and numerous broken chairs, only four of which were useable. Two of the good chairs were occupied by a young couple and there was no one else in the bar so we took the other two bracketing a wobbly table.

We looked about us in puzzlement. An interior architectural motif that had aimed for *flashy-disco* had become *ransacked-garage*.

Eventually a waitress appeared from somewhere and said all they had was beer. We ordered two, drank half, left double the price, and beat it out of there.

Such was the departure lounge at the country's premier tourist destination.

Where does the buck stop, Bob?

7

Pretoria, South Africa – 3 days, self-drive, and Sam's car

Back at the Wilson's we rented a car, went to a couple malls, baked 120 potatoes, boiled four dozen eggs, and loaded a BushBaby trailer with food, clothing and toys.

The rental car was to experience driving another five-speed manual-shift, left-handed, sitting on the right side of the car, staying on the wrong side of the road, with Donna Mae shrieking at me.

The malls were to see exactly how the white folks shop.

The potatoes, eggs and stuff in the trailer were for two braais that we – the Wilsons and the Grays – were putting on Saturday for a jillian kids at two orphanages in the small town of Manzini, in Swaziland. The first braai would be at Menzi's *Enjabulweni*, which Melinda had been telling me about for ten years. The second braai would be at one called *MacCorkindales*, which I had heard about only recently from a good lady who had done volunteer work there thirty-something years ago. I was gratified not just to be paying a naked visit to these two places but also to be able to visit some cheer upon them as well.

The two kids the Wilsons adopted from *Enjabulweni* are grown now, but John and Melinda have remained dedicated to *Enjabulweni* and, by association, also to *MacCorkindales*.

A small percentage of the younger kids at these orphanages are HIV positive as a result of mother-to-child transmission. A greater percentage will become HIV positive beginning in their early teens as they become sexually active. Here the importance of education and prophylactics smacks the newcomer in the face.

The Wilsons' entire professional lives have been dedicated to public health, mostly in Africa. In their free time, they contribute regularly to both *Enjabulweni* and *MacCorkindales*...in ways we in America can't imagine. One of those ways is to visit from time to time with food, clothes and toys.

That was the point of the braais.

While Donna Mae and I were in Zimbabwe and Botswana, John and Melinda had spent an entire weekend buying, cooking, wrapping, and freezing: three 15 lb. beef rumps, 45 lbs. of chicken, 22 lbs. of hot dogs, and 26 lbs. of fat brown sausages called Boerowurst which is supposed to be pork but could easily be horsemeat. In addition, they had assembled enough ancillary items of food and drink to feed the Macedonian army of Alexander The Great.

The Boerowurst looked repulsive and I said so to Melinda. Patiently, she said the kids loved it and it might be the only meat they would taste in a year. Foot was in my mouth again.

While John and Melinda attended to their day jobs, our assignment was to assemble the rest of the stuff – potatoes, eggs, buns, tables, pots, pans, utensils, cookers, etc. – and load the trailer.

Packed into these three days in Pretoria, we found time to visit the *Lion & Rhino Nature Reserve*, a self-drive game park on the outskirts of Jo'burg stocked with lion, cheetah, wild dog, rhino, buffalo, hippo, crocodile, warthog, oryx and springbok.

Sam Wilson, another son, took a day off from work and drove us there in his Subaru 4x4. He was especially keen to show us the noon, lion-feeding in which a ranger in a pick-up truck chains a giant slab of meat to a post in the middle of an open field and nine adult lions materialize from the bushes and rip the meat apart.

"You'll just love it," Sam said. "It's the park's main attraction."

We watched this spectacle with undisguised amazement, photographing from inside the car at about 50 meters. With the car windows down (halfway), the close-up view of lions thus masticating was eerily educational, the unimpeded sound of it haunting.

It is hard to say which was more unsettling though: the sound of bones crushing between snarling teeth or the way the lions materialized from the bushes. There was absolutely no sign of a lion anywhere during a half hour of driving around the place until the truck with meat showed up and instantly there were nine lions strolling towards it. The admonition at self-drive game parks not to get out of the car was graphically underscored.

Then we drove into a separate enclosure and watched a pack of wild dogs rip apart chicken carcasses thrown to them by the rangers.

Then we went to lunch.

After lunch we went into another fenced enclosure that featured two white-lion cubs *and* two tiger cubs, all frolicking *together* in a small pen.

I did a double-take. Something didn't compute. There are no tigers in the wild in Africa. But I had to admit, it was a curious marketing gimmick.

For five rands, a short young lady with a baby on her hip let me go inside the pen. The cubs were so cute, so exotic, so absurdly housed together that just being in with them made me giddy. I was also a little cocky from my encounters with cheetahs and the lion cub from the last safari. I thought I was a great and fearless cat handler.

Without hesitation, I squatted on my haunches and hoisted a tiger and a lion onto my lap for a grand hugging and cuddling and a prize photo op. The tiger cub was the size of a German Shepherd and the lion cub was an ounce smaller. They were happy to be handled, happy to scrabble across my knees and squirm playfully in my lap, oblivious of the play of their claws upon my lily-white skin.

I tried to smooch the tiger but he rejected my affections and instead took a mouthful of tee-shirt at my shoulder. Upon reflection I realized that could have been my ear. I have two but that's not a reason to be careless.

Meanwhile, the lion slipped down my leg and chomped playfully onto my right-foot. I winced.

I was still working stubbornly on the cuddling and the photo op when they both got bored with me and began lurching and twisting. Then teeth were mashing and claws were flying and I was becoming a human chew-toy.

"Apparently you have lost control of the situation," observed Donna Mae sweetly.

"Get the picture, goddammit! Get the picture!" I yelled.

The boys exhibited some reluctance to disengage and she snapped away at a leisurely pace, enjoying my predicament.

"Okay, boys," I said, struggling to my feet, "this has been fun. Aloha!"

I tore away and jumped out of the pen.

"Nice going, Tarzan," said Donna Mae.

But I was ecstatic. What a kick! The smallest of those cubs was to a kitten what a wood-chipper is to a butter knife.

What an indulgence!

Then Sam took us to another game park he said had lions we could get closer to.

He was right. We drove around inside an enclosure containing lion couples and cubs of various ages all running around freely, some right next to the car.

The route through the place was wet and bumpy and Sam tried to negotiate a long muddy pothole that was deeper than it looked. Halfway through the pothole, something dislodged itself with a sharp crack from under the driver-side front fender and dragged along noisily under the car as Sam continued forward.

When the car emerged from the pothole, a three-foot section of a black plastic mudguard popped out onto the ground next to the driver-side front door.

Sam stopped the car, put on the emergency brake, and started out the door to retrieve the mudguard.

Donna Mae noticed that the sharp crack had drawn the attention of a huge male lion out for a stroll with his sweetheart a very few meters to our front.

She let out a shriek heard in Bangkok.

Even the lion flinched.

Sam jumped back, yanked the door closed, and rolled up the window just as the lion pounced on the mudguard.

We all sat there panting, babbling things like, "Holy shit!" and "Jesus Christ!"

The lion chomped on the mudguard and dragged it away about ten feet.

The female joined him, and there in the long dry grass, the happy couple proceeded to tear it to pieces like kittens on cat-nip.

That could have been Sam.

8

Swaziland – 3 days, self-drive, John's car

Friday afternoon, John, Melinda, Donna Mae and I drove six hours to Mbabane, Swaziland in John's Toyota 4-Runner, towing the BushBaby trailer full of all the stuff for the two braais on Saturday.

That night we stayed in a stone mansion operated as a B&B perched on the side of a small mountain with a view that rivaled those we'd seen in the Alps. That part of Swaziland is the Switzerland of Africa.

The meat in the BushBaby was still frozen solid and we needed it to be ready to cook in the morning, so we took all of it out of the trailer and arrayed it around the lip of our marble bathtub to thaw overnight. The absurdity of this did not escape me.

In the morning, the meat now cookable, we headed out to Manzini. About 11:00 AM, we pulled into the yard at *Enjabulweni*. Cedric, Ntamsile, and Menzi were there to greet us. As we started unloading the trailer, a crowd of fifty or sixty kids with eager expressions, ages 2 to 20, surrounded us. We gave them drinks and toys, and articles of clothing we'd brought for this purpose, and cooked about half of the food and served it to them.

They ate everything served. Not one scrap of food was thrown away.

Quite unexpectedly, four of the older boys put on a traditional, costumed, Swazi dance performance to thank us. They dance professionally, which we didn't know at the time but learned only later, confirming an obvious suspicion. It was a powerful, moving performance with sharp drum beat and fierce chanting. They were bare-chested and wore red, blue and yellow wraps around their waist. Their feet and ankles were wrapped with thick white fur, an adornment to accentuate the foot-stomping characteristic throughout southern Africa of this style of aboriginal dance.

A crowd gathered.

Six kids climbed into a small tree behind the dancers and sat there mesmerized through the entire performance.

A few feet to the right of the dancers, two ten-year-old boys mimicked the dancers' moves with stern concentration, practicing for the day when they would enjoy that honor.

We all stood dumbfounded…and brushed away a few tears.

While the dance was going on, I noticed that Cedric had been circling around behind us directing angry expressions at the dancers. I thought someone must have committed some serious transgression, so later I asked Cedric if something was wrong, if someone was in trouble. He smiled and said he was merely admonishing two of the younger dancers who were loafing a bit. Specifically, he said, they were not vigorously executing the stomp, the high knee-rise and emphatic foot-stamp, the most important cultural feature of the dance. Cedric was a proud man, a decent man, he did not want to see either his dancers or *Enjabulweni* embarrassed.

Before we left, the younger teenage boys wanted to show us their rooms. A small group of them led us exuberantly through a nearby, one-story concrete building divided into a warren of small rooms, each housing five or six single beds, dormitory style.

The beds were rickety iron frames that sagged under the weight of thin misshapen mattresses and threadbare sheets. It was hard to imagine how much more they sagged bearing the burden of these children. Not much I guessed. These kids were rail-thin.

Their personal possessions were few and were strewn on the beds or stacked haphazardly nearby. There were no dressers or chests or closets.

The walls were once a lively color, probably the yellow of banana, but now were faded to a mud color and peeling.

The floor was smooth, bare concrete and had been swept cursorily for our visit.

The boys escorted us eagerly, spontaneously; I'm sure they had not been put up to it.

They pointed out every aspect of their existence, their beds, their possessions, the sinks, the toilets, and the shower spigot high in a small enclosure smaller than a phone booth that gave neither hot nor cold, only water.

They had no parents, some were HIV-positive, but they had a roof over their head, four walls, beds, each other, and they had Cedric and *Enjabulweni*, and they were animated and proud of their home, and not alone. They had a foundation upon which to commence a life. The lucky ones would.

About 2:30 we packed up the trailer for the drive across town to put on another braai at *MacCorkindales*.

Cedric, Menzi, and the lead *Enjabulweni* dancer named Ncamiso wanted to come along so we squeezed them into the 4-Runner with us and set off.

I sat next to Ncamiso and struck up a conversation. A few years earlier, he had been one of those younger lads who had just shown us their quarters. I was surprised by his stunningly charming personality and perfect command of the English language. He said he was just finishing high school and dearly wished to continue his education at the college level. It was heartening to see a successful product of *Enjabulweni's* succor. In the short drive across Manzini we didn't get too deeply into the details of how he would go about furthering his education, but his enthusiasm was so genuine that I asked for his mailing address, hoping he would indeed pursue his goal and wondering how I might encourage his efforts to do so.

A few minutes later, with Cedric's help, we found the long dirt track leading up a slight incline to *MacCorkindales*.

As John started up the track, Cedric pointed to a kraal (group of small huts, or mini village, of native Africans) set on the low hill off to our left, a quarter-mile from the entrance to *MacCorkindales*. He said the kraal housed a couple dozen very poor kids who would also be very hungry.

Without hesitation, John took a left-turn leading to the kraal, pulled up onto a bare patch of dirt between two small buildings and cut the engine.

Instantly, a crowd of small, ragged half-naked kids materialized around the 4-Runner. The look of astonishment on their faces was the same look you would see on the faces of kids in Ohio if a space ship landed in their schoolyard. Kids are kids the world over.

The kids were followed immediately by an old lady waving away a cloud of dust and frowning skeptically, unsure if we were friend or foe.

The familiar faces of Cedric and Menzi sitting amongst us probably saved the old lady from cardiac arrest. Cedric explained to her that we had come to put on a braai at *MacCorkindales* and they were invited. The lady in turn explained that to the kids and they cheered wildly.

Donna Mae, Ncamiso and I jumped out of the 4-Runner and played Pied Piper, leading the kids down the track to *MacCorkindales* while John and the others drove on ahead.

I've never seen a happier bunch of kids.

I've never seen a hungrier bunch of kids either.

When John pulled into the yard at *MacCorkindales* there were no adults about so Melinda went looking through the main building. She found the headmistress napping in a far bedroom and woke her up with the good news that we had just arrived to put on a party in the yard for the whole orphanage and all the kids from the neighboring kraal.

The lady was grumpier than one might expect upon being so informed. She claimed she had the flu, and suggested it was not a good day for such an event.

"Oh but it is," said Melinda, in her sweetest and most authoritative tone.

And so it was.

We set up our tables and cook stoves next to where John had parked in the yard, a flat clearing beside a small hill. The hillside was a backdrop upon which some of the kids sat and watched the crazy white folks at work.

We did a repeat of the earlier braai, this one a lot smoother owing to a practiced routine and the pre-sundowners I was forced to break out.

There was no professional dance group there to provide entertainment, but a guy named Spencer, who owns the kraal and maintains it with his own funds, pulled his car into the yard and blasted out music to the delight of the kids.

Spencer was an orphan, raised at *MacCorkindales,* and now as a successful businessman he has a special dedication to the place. He is intimately familiar with the dusty yard there and the rare instances of compassion that brighten a child's day.

I put five of our folding chairs at the base of the hill at a central point that overlooked the festivities and Melinda badgered the grumpy headmistress out of her room and into the middle chair. Donna Mae put the old lady from the kraal and her husband on one side, and Cedric and Spencer on the other, subtly making the headmistress the obvious guest of honor.

As the braai progressed and everyone was being fed, I noticed the headmistress's expression was mellowing and she was in danger of enjoying herself. I kept looking over at her, making faces until she could no longer withhold the flicker of a smile.

I pointed at her.

"Aha, I see that," I said, loudly for everyone to hear.

She could restrain herself no longer, and broke out in wide grin.

I ran over, and with an exaggerated motion made a show of planting a big juicy kiss on her face. She blushed like a school girl and everyone within a mile radius burst out laughing.

So there was a happy ending to her day after all.

And the braai was another big hit. Every remaining morsel of food was consumed.

By 6:30, we were packed up and gone like a tribe of Bedouins.

We got back to Mbabane about 8:00, drag-ass tired, found an Indian restaurant, patted ourselves on the back, and killed two bottles of Spier sauvignon blanc. We figured we had fed about 150 kids and a few adults.

There are not many adults in attendance at these orphanages in Swaziland. Those that are should be beatified.

The next day we went on a mid-day, game drive in the Mkhaye Nature Reserve located in central Swaziland. The day was sunny and the drive in an open vehicle was hot and uncomfortable. We saw plenty of rhino, elephant, hippo, giraffe, impala, nyala, warthog, and one lousy croc.

At a point none too soon, the driver asked if everyone had seen enough. All heads bobbed in the affirmative and the driver headed back to the reception area. There, to our great relief, we were served a fine lunch at tables primly set in the coolness of billowing shade trees. We dined in splendor while a family of nyala strolled between the tables as if we weren't there.

It is amazing in Africa, and sometimes unsettling, how quickly you can go from discomfort to bliss, or paucity to surfeit, or both.

Leaving the game reserve, John drove due north an interminable distance, to the top of a mountain at a place called Siteki. He parked in some bushes and he and Melinda took off through high weeds following a densely overgrown path. I didn't know what the hell was going on, but Donna Mae was right behind them and sensing an event of some moment, I hoisted the cooler onto my shoulders and followed after them.

After 100 meters or so, the path opened out onto a massive out-cropping of granite, a sparkling grey precipice sitting pristine, two-thousand feet above a green valley floor spread below as far as the eye could see. Donna Mae stopped dead in her tracks, startled and incredulous. I caught up to her as she was saying, "Holy shit!"

John and Melinda skipped out onto the granite out-cropping like kids at a day camp. John took Melinda by the hand and they eased over to the very edge of the precipice, to the exact spot they were married 34 years ago. It was their first return in ten years. They kissed and we all cried.

I was never so happy to have a loaded cooler at hand.

Then they joined us on safer ground and we broke out the sundowners and sat there on the bare rock for an hour or so and got loaded.

Donna Mae and I sat some yards apart from the happy couple, allowing them their private reflections. We were so blown away by the majestic view we could have sat there all day.

Eventually we all got up and took a bunch of photos – Donna Mae took a dozen of the setting sun alone.

Then we drove back to Mbabane to our B&B.

In the morning, the BushBaby trailer in tow, we left the B&B and set off to visit Agnes. Before heading up the hill to Agnes's kraal, John stopped at a Total petrol station to fill up the gas tank and for Melinda to meet clandestinely with the sister of an HIV patient.

Melinda had taken another dying African under her wing. Some days before, she had insisted that the patient be admitted forthwith to a Johannesburg hospital where there was a chance her life could be saved with a three-drug, antiretroviral regimen. The patient was in such poor condition that an airline would not carry her and so she had been transported from Swaziland to the hospital in the back of a pick-up truck. In hospital, she underwent the drug regimen and was showing signs of improvement when her mother came and removed her from the hospital, claiming she was bringing shame upon the family. Melinda was determined to save the patient and so had arranged to get the drug regimen to her through her sister, unbeknownst to the mother.

While John stretched out the act of filling the gas tank, Melinda and the sister sat talking at a picnic bench in the shade next to the petrol station. Melinda had brought the antiretroviral drugs from the hospital to give to the sister to administer. The details of administering the drug regimen were complicated and delicate, and if the regimen were not completed exactly as prescribed, it would be of no use whatsoever. It was essential, therefore, for Melinda to deliver precise instructions *to* the sister and to insure that they were understood as such *by* the sister. Under this circumstance, time was not relevant to Melinda, only effective communication was. So we waited.

Finally satisfied, Melinda hugged the sister, said goodbye, and returned to the car wiping tears from her eyes.

We left the petrol station and John drove up into the hills above Mbabane on a winding gravel track to Agnes's kraal. Over the course of many years, Agnes had been nanny to three Wilson kids and to an infant the eldest Wilson daughter had adopted from an orphanage in KwaZulu-Natal. John and Melinda revere Agnes. They would not come to Swaziland without visiting her.

Agnes is 57 but looks like 77. She has the heart of a teenager, and cares only for her life of servitude. She lives with her daughters and their kids in a small dark house in a meadow in the hills. Her kraal.

A stone-throw away, a half-built house sits baking in the late morning sun. It is Agnes's dream house. Now it is just a shell of concrete-block looking more abandoned than unfinished. Doors, windows and roof have not been added yet. Agnes waits to accumulate enough money someday to have these items installed so a concrete floor can be poured and she can move in. I asked Melinda if we could send her money for that and she said Agnes would not use it for that purpose, she would just give it to her kids.

Her house would never be finished.

The saddest dreams are those still-born.

Agnes and her youngest daughter and another lady greeted us as we pulled into the yard. There was a round of introductions and hugging and tears, after which John opened the trailer and Melinda distributed various items of food, clothing, and toys, stuff they had packed in Pretoria and had kept aside just for this purpose.

Three of Agnes's grandchildren, ages 5, 4 and 3, stood by transfixed, showing no movement or emotion until lollipops and a soccer ball appeared. That perked them up and started their part of the party.

The emotion in the meadow got even heavier at that point as Melinda and John reminisced with their beloved Agnes. Donna Mae and I withdrew to give them their privacy and spent the rest of the visit kicking the soccer ball around with the kids.

Before we departed, Agnes implored us to walk with her through the small dark house. We entered through a tiny kitchen bereft of electricity or appliances and passed through to a warren of small bedrooms, unlit and claustrophobic to the western experience. There were blankets strewn about on several small beds but no toys or playthings in evidence. Walls were bare. There was no living room or other area for the family to gather. Nevertheless, Agnes escorted us proudly, gesturing to beds and chairs and items of clothing as if she had read our mind about the fruitless effort to build her future house and needed to assure us that in spite of it she and her family were all quite well.

There was no question the kids kicking the soccer ball around were quite well.

The joke was on me; anyone cared for by Agnes would be...quite well.

Down from the hills, we drove through the Ezulwini Valley – a popular artsy-craftsy tourist route linking Mbabane with Manzini – to buy candles and gifts.

Along the way, John stopped at a place called St. Mary's Mission, to allow Melinda a few moments of reflection. As a 19-year-old college drop-out, she had come to Africa on her own and had spent her first year here teaching school before returning to Illinois to get a Ph.D. in public health.

The place was a smaller version of a typical church school. Several weathered, one-story stucco buildings with faded, green tile roofs dotted a small campus, the lawns spare and minimally tended. A small cross sat at the apex of the largest building.

It was mid-day of a Sunday afternoon and nobody seemed to be about.

Melinda pointed nostalgically to her dormitory building, a worn concrete structure the size and shape of a single-wide mobile home. It housed a row of small individual rooms accessed along one side by steel-frame doors with lever handles.

"There was a small sink in each room," she explained, "and a single toilet in a tiny hut down that path over there alongside the building."

"That's it?" I asked.

"Yup!" she said, laughing. "You'd be surprised how much washing you can do in a small sink and how fast you can make it down that path."

"What did you do here?"

"I taught math to the kids," she said, laughing more heartily at the recollection. "I had trouble with math in high school and here I was teaching it."

"How'd you manage that?"

"Well, you can be sure I didn't ask for that. I arrived to do volunteer work and they just assigned me to it. But it really wasn't hard teaching math to kids who hadn't even learned to count yet."

"Oh!"

It didn't take a genius to see where her lifelong commitment and devotion to an ideal had begun. And *why* it had begun.

Continuing on, we made several stops at craft shops, and on schedule at 1:00 PM, John found the car-hire place at the Manzini airport where I had booked a rental car for the remainder of our trip: a self-drive safari through the KwaZulu-Natal Province of South Africa.

We said our goodbyes and Donna Mae and I set off on our own, heading southwest across Swaziland towards the border post at Lavumisa. The car was a pint-size VW Golf identical to the replacement car that had gotten the four of us back to Windhoek from Sosussvlei two weeks earlier.

It would be inaccurate to say we were relieved to leave the emotion of Swaziland behind us because we were not. Thanks to Melinda and John we had experiences that cannot be bought or ever duplicated, and for that we were grateful and in a state of greater peace. We shared our thoughts for a few hours as we wound through verdant hills, slowing occasionally to pass groups of uniformed school children walking home along the side of the road. Farther south, the road flattened and straightened, homesteads became fewer and vegetation sparse. Gradually we got ourselves focused on our next adventure.

Lavumisa was hot and dusty, no reason we could see for it being there other than as a border post. Thankfully, there was a tiny market where I was able to get a couple bottles of water. A half-dozen small block buildings were scattered randomly on either side of the road. There was no vegetation for miles around.

There were only two other people in line with us leaving Swaziland. The process was swift and painless. Both countries' border officials were eager to pass all of us through quickly so they could go back to reading their magazines.

Before crossing the magic line into South Africa, however, a handsome twenty-something border guard politely inquired who we preferred in the coming election, Hillary or Obama. I said Hillary, Donna Mae said Obama.

The chap was aghast. "He's Kenyan," he blurted.

Donna Mae jumped on him. "He certainly is not. His father was Kenyan. He was born and raised in America. According to *our* law, he's an American."

"Oh!"

He raised the bar and let us into South Africa anyway.

9

Zululand, South Africa – 5 days, self-drive, rental car

Exiting Swaziland, we picked up the N2, the spanking-clean, national highway leading from Pretoria and Jo'burg down to the resort beaches along the Indian Ocean coastline of KwaZulu-Natal province.

Our destination was the *Bayete Zulu Lodge*, a 4-star, fully-catered, weekend kind of place with only 8 rooms. It was advertised as lavishly appointed in Zulu motifs and easily accessible by personal 2x4 vehicle. I had booked it on-line and now we had to find it. The directions were to proceed down the N2 "about" 90 kilometers from the Swaziland border, turn right at the Total petrol station just past Mkuze, and follow the gravel road for 9 kilometers to a clearly marked main entrance. This I did.

We had been on the road for about 5 hours so I had a little trepidation about finding the place in the dark. As it turned out, there was still plenty of light and the approach to the lodge was a mini game-drive in itself. Nyala, impala and warthog dithered along the gravel track, deigning to move aside only at the last second. A Black Rhino ambled by in the meadow below the reception just as we pulled up in front of it.

The *Bayete Zulu Lodge* privately owns 5,700 of the 54,000 acres comprising the Zululand Rhino Reserve. By agreement, *Bayete* and only a few other land-owning lodges are licensed to conduct game-drives throughout the entire reserve. The terrain is a varied landscape of low mountains, open plains and riverine woodlands. The reserve is stocked with elephant, rhino, cape buffalo, hippo, crocodile, ostrich, warthog, impala, nyala, and kudu. Other than the few lodges and the gravel tracks used for the game drives, there is no other sign of human presence there.

We were there at mid-week and the place was slow. There was one other couple, a real estate developer from Cape Town with a big-hair wife and two kids. The wife was remote, the kids were cute. The guy was initially reserved, almost to the point of rudeness, but on the second day when I encountered him after breakfast, he became surprisingly chatty.

He had a digital camera around his neck and had just returned from an early morning game-drive. He scrolled through the view-finder and showed me a series of photos he had taken, photos he was quite proud of. They were all of trees. I thought the poor chap must be mad. He said his hobby was taking photos of trees for his wife to paint. At that I was convinced he was mad.

For his wife to paint? What are the odds of those two finding each other? That such a fate did not happen to me reminded me of the Christian expression: *Thank you, Lord. Thank you, Jesus.*

We went on two mid-day, game drives but didn't see much wildlife. The guides were perhaps the most articulate we had encountered and they made the drives enjoyable by expounding knowledgeably on trees, bugs, weather, wildlife, and all things bush.

We learned that the famous fever tree that grows in low-lying areas was misnamed by early settlers who thought it was the cause of malaria. Eventually they learned the culprit was the mosquito that just happens to live in the same habitat.

We also learned that the iconic, flat-topped tree seen everywhere and associated romantically with Africa is the umbrella acacia; that the big gobs of rhino dung are territorial markings left by dominant males; that at night hippos may forage several kilometers from their waterhole and will instantly dispatch any living creature – especially human – witless enough to block their return path; that the various dead trees we'd seen interspersed with live ones died because the elephants stripped off their bark; that the adolescent male impala hangs around in an all-boy herd until he becomes big enough to drive off the sole stud from a family-herd and become the sole stud himself with the job to bonk all the ladies in the herd until he in turn gets driven off, and the wheel keeps turning; and that this dominant male-bull theme seems to run through most of the four-legged mammalian species, albeit in varying degrees of sociability.

The ostrich specie handles these things differently. Coming upon a group of three in a sparsely wooded field, we noticed the middle ostrich spinning frantically, pirouetting, as if trying to fling fleas from his feathers (try that quickly). The crazy bird did this for a full two minutes. I thought it was having a fit, so I turned to our guide. "What's that about?" I asked.

"That's a courtship dance," he said proudly, eager to display his knowledge of the bush. "It's a dance to attract a female. That group, they're all young males, and that one is practicing his dance in front of his buddies. You're lucky; this is a very rare sight."

Quick thinking, I thought, to come up with that piece of bullshit.

But I wondered anyway. I tried to work it out as if it were true. Let's say I grant the *very rare* part. But how about the *in front of his buddies* part? Would they critique him? Would they advise him? It didn't make sense. Why would his buddies want to help him become the best dancer and ace them out of the hottest ostrich chick?

Bush queries.

Our last game drive was at night. It was just me and Donna Mae and the real estate developer family. We saw very little wildlife although the driver did his best to find some utilizing a spotlight with a lens the diameter of a hubcap powered by the vehicle's battery. It was full dark, no moon, and the thing lit up the night like a search-light at a Hollywood premiere. I have always found this practice counter-intuitive. Shouldn't it would freak the wildlife which we are always instructed not to disturb with loud talk and quick movements? But under questioning, the driver merely said, "Nah, it doesn't bother them a bit." How'd he know that, I wondered. Probably took the course: *Compassionate Jack-Lighting of African Wildlife*.

In spite of the driver's good-faith efforts – or maybe because of – the wildlife seemed to have disappeared. I'm guessing even the dumbest of them, upon hearing the vehicle's approach, withdrew smartly into the darkness.

But the drive was not a bust. Returning to the lodge, we came upon the resident herd of cape buffalo, grazing in the track blocking our path. The driver tried to inch the truck forward but the herd wasn't budging so we sat there for a while in the dark to quietly observe their movements.

The big-hair wife got impatient and barked at the driver from the back seat, "Oh just go through them, they'll move."

I was amused by this outburst, wondering how the driver would react. Even the most dull-witted tourist eventually learns it is inadvisable and potentially unhealthy to startle certain of the wildlife species with a shrill utterance.

The driver surprised me by his forbearance.

"Shut the f#?k up!" is what he should have said, but he was a gentleman and merely said, "Shhhh!"

Then the main bull started drifting back through the trees alongside us as if to get behind the truck. The driver backed up slowly to match the bull's movements, whispering softly what the bull was up to: "Ambush is a standard buffalo tactic. He will try to appear disinterested in order to sneak behind us and charge into our vehicle."

With that we all sat quietly. Even the big-hair wife.

After a few tense minutes of playing match-the-buffalo, the bull lost interest and wandered off, taking the herd with him. He was one big cow and would have scattered the lot of us from the truck if he had charged into it.

The driver wiped his brow.

"Drink time," I whispered to Donna Mae.

"Yebow!" she answered in the local vernacular.

After two nights at the *Bayete Zulu Lodge*, we continued south down the N2 to the town of Hluhluwe. You think Sosussvlei is hard to say, try that. The best version I heard was *shloo-shlooey*, so I went with that, though it must have been wrong because when I said it people looked at me piteously like I had a speech defect. Fortunately, we found the place clearly sign-posted without having to ask for it by name.

In the small town center, I found a Spar Market to replenish our snacks and essential beverages. I pulled up in front and Donna Mae hopped out and went into the store. I parked in a stall next to a low wall.

As I got out of the car two barefoot, half-naked kids sitting on the wall asked to look at the car.

"Sure," I said, holding the door open and gesturing at the interior. "Pretty nice, huh? Have a look."

They didn't move from the low wall; they just stared at me like I had three heads.

"I guess they're not impressed," I mumbled to myself as I locked the door and headed for the market.

Two steps inside the door it hit me. I had misunderstood them. They weren't asking to look *at* the car, they were asking to look *after* the car, as is a custom in South Africa. This was, of course, notwithstanding that they were all of 8 years old. Nevertheless, I felt pretty stupid. I could picture them sharing a laugh: *old-geezer-can't-hear-shit*.

I found Donna Mae and tried to explain to her what I had just done. All I got for that was the look: *old-geezer-can't-hear-shit*.

She was way in the back part of the store perusing the aisles and I noticed that the kinds of goods on display there had transitioned from the bulk items at the front where we had entered – bags of flour, corn and sugar, tins of oil, loose vegetables – to more discretionary items, cheeses, chips, mixers, wines.

Farther back, on the left side of the store, I noticed another "front" entrance, outside of which was another parking lot. In that lot were parked up-scale, late model cars and SUVs. Sonofabitch! I wondered once again at my stupidity.

"Donna Mae," I called, a bit louder than necessary, "isn't that the old, white folks' entrance, a remnant of South Africa's shameful and not-too-distant past? Wouldn't that make the one we used the *kaffirs'* entrance?"

"Brilliant observation, Einstein."

"Well, shit!" I said. "The way we came in is good enough for us; besides it's closer to our car."

Before leaving the cheese and wine section, I added two bottles of Coca Cola to our pile of purchases.

We finished shopping, paid our bill and walked out.

The two kids were still sitting on the wall waiting to mind somebody's car. I handed each of them a bottle of Coke, which they accepted hesitantly. I suspected no one had ever done that before. But they remained expressionless, with even more reason to appraise me like I had three heads.

"Okay, okay," I muttered, mostly for my own benefit. "Goddamn kids sure know how to work an old man. I know what you're waiting for. Here, here, take it all." I gave them all the rands in my pocket, a little more than a buck

As I pulled away, they were sitting in the same spot on the wall drinking their Cokes. Finally they were smiling.

Continuing on to the *Bonamanzi Game Park* required circumnavigating four roundabouts and trundling 6 km. down a gravel road and across a deep wash that would be under 8 feet of water in a heavy downpour. Fortunately it was a sunny day.

The *Bonamanzi Game Park* is a 10,000 acre, private game reserve offering a variety of accommodations such as ensuite rooms, lodges, tree-houses, and campsites. I had booked a self-catering tree-house for the convenience of a small kitchen, although we would take our meals at the lodge's open-air restaurant.

A pretty young African woman who spoke the King's English checked us in at reception. I asked her how to pronounce Hluhluwe and she did so, employing the click consonant associated mostly with the San (Bushman) language but common in Zulu as well. I asked her to repeat it two more times and she did. Then I tried it. But it was impossible; I couldn't get it for love or money. She laughed at me politely. When I said I had heard white folks pronounce it *shloo-shlooey*, she laughed again, heartily, like whiteys are retarded. She meant no disrespect and I took none. We had a good yuck and returned to the King's English. I guess she thought I was a nice old man because she gave us the best tree-house, No. 10, at the end of the line, tucked away in the trees, out of sight of any humans or man-made objects. Or maybe she thought that's where I belonged.

The tree-house was set on round poles, the floor of it about ten feet from the ground. It was one big room, delightfully rustic, with a sort of high-sierra, pine décor – everything, walls, ceiling, floor, and furniture was pine. There was a tiny kitchen with pine cabinetry, a large pine-walled bathroom, and a wide pine deck that looked out through the trees towards a dry riverbed frequented by a family of impala.

A mother and two adolescent impala nibbling at the ground on the banks of the riverbed ignored me as I unloaded the car.

We were magnificently alone.

I sat naked on the deck, enjoying a cool drink and contemplating a family of vervet monkeys chattering in the trees at eye level.

Donna Mae yelled from inside the house, "Put some clothes on."

"I'm bonding with our simian cousins here," I said, but the damage was done. The monkeys had vanished.

Dinner that night was another braai, located at the end of the road a mile or so past our tree-house, serving to begin after dark, amongst candles and campfire. The instructions were to *drive to the braai*. Some rules just *feel* like good rules. In Africa, those are the kind you just *feel* like following.

Again, impala, kudu and warthog were the featured delicacies. Donna Mae didn't seem to have any problem with the impala even though some of the little guys had been grazing under our tree house an hour earlier.

The next day we went on a two-hour walking safari with a guide named Bernie, a robust white-Zimbabwean lady, dressed nattily from head to toe in khaki safari garb.

Quite wisely, she had left her country to find employment. She had grown up in the bush and knew more about wildlife than Marlin Perkins.

We walked along animal trails, through thickets and scrub, past a bleached buffalo skull lying in the sand, towards the open plains beyond. The sun shone weakly, soothing the air, but not baking it.

Bernie was ebullient, explaining the tracks in the sand and the critters that made them. Suddenly she reached down, and like a kid picking up a marble, snatched up a large black, dung beetle the size of a Blackberry. Donna Mae jumped back a foot as Bernie turned it upside down and pointed to a tic lodged in the beetle's abdomen.

"Few people know this," she said with a smile, "but the tic is really what leads the beetle to the dung."

"So," I said, "without the tic, the beetle can't find shit?"

I thought myself a great wit and laughed heartily.

Donna Mae gave me a dirty look.

Bernie must have figured two can play that game.

"The *Bonamanzi Game Park* has the largest rock python population in Zululand," she said, deadpan.

I gasped. Somehow she divined that I am not a snake person.

Then she pointed to the ground where I was standing and showed me a long, slim track in the sand. "That's where one of the buggers slithered across the path into the undergrowth," she said, "quite recently."

This time I jumped back a foot. That bit of intelligence would haunt me for the rest of our stay there.

We continued on, out onto open plains where no farther away than the length of a tennis court, small herds of zebra, wildebeest and impala grazed in the warm sun. No larger mammals were about but it did not diminish the experience.

We passed a pond that was supposed to have a croc in it but didn't see one. I didn't think it necessary to go poking around trying to confirm the fact. I'm comfortable with certain advice.

It was a leisurely stroll, uneventful by Africa standards, but it felt good to be on the ground for a change, not sitting high in a vehicle – even with crocs lurking and pythons on the loose.

Later that afternoon, Bernie found me gawking at the thirteen monstrous crocs basking in the sun on the lawn of a fenced enclosure behind the reception building.

"Why are all their mouths wide open?" I asked her.

"That's their air-conditioning system," she answered. "They're cooling themselves off."

Then she dashed into a back room and reappeared a minute later for show-and-tell, holding a plastic bucket with an 18-inch baby croc in it. Its teeth were too sharp for even her to risk grabbing it, so she pinned its head down with a stick and picked it up by its neck. It thrashed and squirmed and when she held it up I could see it didn't like me…or her either.

"A croc lays about 80 eggs," she said. "Only about 50 of them hatch, and only one makes it to adulthood. The rest get eaten by predators."

Bad odds for crocs, I thought, good for humans.

It had been a wonderful day, and I was feeling so giddy from being close to mother earth that I booked a three-hour horseback safari for noon the next day.

Back at the tree-house, I broke the news to Donna Mae.

"What's that exactly?" she said, for the second time on our trip.

"We each ride our own horse, and a guide on another horse leads us around," I said enthusiastically. "It's easier than riding a bike with trainer wheels. The guide will take us right out onto the plains...amongst the wildlife. How cool is that?"

"Cool?" she said skeptically. "In the noon-day sun?"

"Uhh...that's when they scheduled it," I said lamely.

"Do we have to?"

"No, we can spend our last day in the African bush sitting on our ass."

"Well, okay," she said, "since you put it so eloquently."

"There's a sport."

That night, I dreamt a python swallowed Donna Mae whole and from its gullet she let out a piercing primordial scream that so startled the beast he snapped inside-out like the crack of a bullwhip.

At noon the next day we met our guide and our horses. The guide was a courteous chap, tall and plump, looking more like a symphony conductor than a cowboy. But he knew his stuff and gave us the tenderfoot's introduction to our horses and the tenderfoot's instruction on steering and braking. We had both ridden a half dozen times in California but had never really gotten the hang of it so we were glad to have the lesson again.

The horses were beautifully groomed, strong, docile, and blessedly obedient.

We set off. The guide made minor corrections to our handling, and in mere minutes we were in the groove, the horses responding perfectly to our touch. It was exhilarating. It was also nice – for once – to have a horse I could steer.

The day was glorious and I had that singing feeling again. I started, "Back in the saddle again—"

"—Don't start," interrupted Donna Mae.

"—out where a friend is a—"

"—Knock it off.

"—friend."

The guide missed it and continued his spiel as we poked along.

"The horses are accustomed to the wildlife and vice-versa," he said. "So we will be able to mosey out onto the plain and mingle with the impala, zebra and wildebeest, the ones you probably saw from a distance yesterday."

We did exactly that and I thought I had died and gone to heaven. To be among them was an inexpressible joy. The difference between *seeing* African wildlife and *being with it* was palpable.

But this nirvana did not prevent me from supposing an obvious corollary: one mustn't wander about in the bush without considering the predators. So when we stopped to rest the horses and were strolling around on the plain like it was the *Jardin des Tuileries*, I asked the guide about the park's predators.

"Any lions in here?"

"No, sir."

"Hyenas?"

"No, sir."

"Wild dogs?"

"No, sir, only a few black-backed jackals, some crocs and the occasional leopard."

"Whoa, that last?" I said.

He smiled a knowing smile and said, "We don't *keep* any in here. But leopards go where they want. Fences don't mean anything to them. Sometimes they come in. You won't see them now; they're nocturnal. They hunt in the dark."

Recalling the story about the unlucky lady that went out walking one night at the Pretoriuskop RestCamp, I chanced to ask, "Anybody ever get eaten here?"

"Not yet."

Oh, that's wonderful: Leopards roaming about freely and the Python Capital of the World. Those thoughts do, however, bring one thing into clearer focus.

Drive to the braai.

We left the bush at 8:00 the next morning and drove three hours down the N2 to Durban, South Africa's third largest city. The bush part of the safari was over and bush withdrawal dogged us like a hangover, dampening an otherwise glorious Zululand day. It's an affliction you won't get departing Tuscany.

For no other reason than to prolong the trip, we sought out one last destination, the famous beachfront of Durban.

A busy main thoroughfare ran in front of chock-a-block, high-rise hotels, their architecture reminiscent of Waikiki Beach *circa* 1950. I found a parking stall in a wide median divider and locked the doors as we got out. An unofficial black man in a tattered shirt hanging around the line of parked cars looked over at me expectantly. I nodded to him and he nodded back. My nod was to accept his unspoken request to watch our car in return for a few rands. It's a South African custom that catches you by surprise the first time, but you get used to it quickly. At 10 rands to the dollar, a gratuity of 5 rands is considered more than adequate. Or so I've been told by white folks.

We walked along a mile of African craft stalls lining the beachfront sidewalk and finally found the small Shona stone figurine Donna Mae had wanted since Zimbabwe, a final happiness to cushion a sad goodbye.

When we returned to the car, the man who was supposed to be watching it was gone so I gave the rands to a cheerful Indian taxi driver in return for directions to the Durban airport.

With no more dawdling, and our last sight seen, we went there, turned in the rental car, and flew back to Jo'burg.

Game over.

But it's not; a part of me is always there in the bush, especially when I'm in a courtroom.

10

Postscript No. 1 – 2009

The good people of Zimbabwe continue to suffer.

The elections in March 2008 were both presidential and parliamentary. Mugabe lost the presidential, and his party, *ZANU-PF,* lost the parliamentary. Although results were posted at the polling places showing Mugabe had lost, the official results were not announced by the Zimbabwe Electoral Commission (located in Harare and controlled by *ZANU-PF*) for some five weeks. Mugabe's vote counters finally confirmed that Morgan Tsvangirai had won. But wait, not by at least 50% plus one as required by Zimbabwe law for outright victory. There would need to be a run-off election...proclaimed Mugabe.

Magic!

He had found a way to win when he had lost.

It was brilliant.

It was criminal, but it was brilliant.

The new election was scheduled for June. In preparation, *ZANU-PF* launched a reign of terror, harassing, intimidating, beating and even killing *MDC* supporters. So blatant, brutal, visible, and widespread were these atrocities that Tsvangirai withdrew from the election, saving countless lives.

That left Mugabe the only candidate.

A monkey can win that kind of election.

He did.

And dig this: his vote count magically soared.

In March, he got 1.08 million votes.

In June, he got 2.15 million votes.

Holy crap! His popularity doubled in three months?

What a man! What a politician!

What a petty little tyrant!

He couldn't settle for a million or so votes from those who would vote for him again. Not this Bob. He had to make a statement. He had to show them who's the boss. He had to have *everyone's* vote.

How this was accomplished is a monument to marketing – and to depravity in the bargain. Everyone was required to vote. Upon doing so, their index finger was dipped in red indelible ink as evidence. Anyone not bearing the red finger stood to lose it. Great motivating factor.

You have to give Mugabe credit for cojones.

He pulled this trick in broad daylight, looked the world squarely in the eye, and as much as said, "Kiss my ass! It's my country and I'll do what I want."

And to compound the tragedy, nobody did jack-shit about it.

He had done it again. He had cheated his own people…again.

Let's not give him all of the credit however. He did not do it alone. That is the other part of the tragedy. He did it in full partnership with those service chiefs, police, and *ZANU-PF* big-wigs who had been living fat off of his tenure, profiting from the land redistribution scheme, siphoning funds from the diamond industry, abusing the human rights of their citizens, ignoring the democratic process, and otherwise openly abusing the rule of law. These were the folks personally responsible for the vote rigging, the reign of terror, and the red-finger debasement.

Why would they do that to their own people? Because they had no choice. They had to keep Mugabe in power and thus maintain their own positions in order to save their own hides from the retribution that would surely follow a Mugabe loss...not to mention a free trip to The Hague for some.

This time, however, Mugabe did not have the hearts of the people. He had finally exhausted his political capital. Everybody on the planet knew the election was a sham and a farce. His own party knew that the election was illegitimate. More to the point, he did not have a majority in parliament and therefore would not be able to form a government. Reluctantly, he realized he would have to reach some accommodation with Morgan Tsvangirai and the *MDC*. And if he could do so under the auspices of the two regional intergovernmental powers, the Southern African Development Community (SADC) and the African Union (AU), he could, if not actually legitimize his presidency, at least have it anointed and preserved for a period of time until he could figure out how to have another election, one he could steal outright.

Outmaneuvered again, the *MDC* settled for what it could get: a "power-sharing" arrangement with *ZANU-PF*, brokered by the SADC and the AU, to form a government of national unity in which Mugabe would remain president and Morgan Tsvangirai would become the Prime Minister. A similar power-sharing government had been formed after political violence marred the aftermath of 2007 elections in Kenya, setting a disturbing precedent for aging incumbent presidents refusing to cede power after being voted out of office.

In that context, it is understandable why the *MDC* wrangled with *ZANU-PF* for months over the structure of such an inclusive government. They finally reached an agreement in September 2008, known as the Global Political Agreement (the GPA). In February 2009, the inclusive government was finally formed.

The GPA provided, amongst other things, that *MDC* would have one more ministry than *ZANU-PF*. But Mugabe had enough muscle to unilaterally grab key ministries, such as Defense, State Security, and Foreign Affairs, thus remaining totally in power.

How did he *grab* ministries, you might ask? Easy. He already owned them. Bought and paid for. All he had to do was say the words Woody Hayes must've said a thousand times: "Okay boys, back in the game."

Also, without consulting his Prime Minister as was required by the GPA, he re-appointed his go-to boys, Gideon Gono as Governor of the RBZ and Johannes Tomana as Attorney General.

Mugabe was conciliatory only so long as it took to maneuver into the GPA and remain President. Since then, there have been too many cases where consultation with the Prime Minister is required by the GPA and he has reverted to his old style, unilaterally appointing judges, ambassadors, provincial governors, and other senior government officials. In doing so, he openly insults Morgan Tsvangirai and cares not a fig what the AU, the SADC, the ANC, Jacob Zuma, Ian Kama, or the Dalai Lama think.

It should now be obvious to the most obtuse observer that the opinions of Mugabe's veracity expressed to me so fervently by ordinary citizens in Victoria Falls on the eve of Election Day were dead on. He never intended to share power with Morgan Tsvangirai. What he could not get through the front door he would reclaim through the back door: power, position, perks, presidential mansion, and the shiny black Rolls-Royce limousine to bear him ceremoniously through the squalid streets of his empire to the opening of parliament where he could punch his little fists in the air and rail against the western powers who caused him to cause that squalor.

For all intents and purposes, Robert Mugabe remains the Emperor of Zimbabwe.

And his *ZANU-PF* loyalists continue to harass and intimidate *MDC* supporters while *ZANU-PF*-controlled police arrest elected *MDC* politicians on trumped-up charges.

And state-sponsored thugs continue to invade the handful of remaining white-owned commercial farms. Land redistribution, my ass.

Thanks to Robert Mugabe, Zimbabwe is a politically rotten place, rotten as pawpaws putrefying in the afternoon sun.

It is a tragedy of astounding proportions.

And the good people of Zimbabwe continue to suffer.

For those interested in background information far more literate and comprehensive than that provided here, I recommend three exceptional, non-fiction books: *The Fear – The Last Days of Robert Mugabe*, by Peter Godwin, published in 2010, W*hen The Crocodile Eats The Sun*, also by Peter Godwin, published in 2006; and *African Laughter – Four Visits To Zimbabwe*, by Doris Lessing, published in 1992.

11

Postscript No. 2 – 2010

Simon, the night watchman at Sossusvlei, is back on his family farm in Mariental, working it with his brothers. I got him to set up a bank account into which money can be deposited from time to time.

In an email to MaryBeth on the subject, I had expressed a concern about knowing whether the funds were being used properly. Perhaps I should request photos or status reports?

MaryBeth is a person of faith, secular as well as religious. Her life's work is proof of her faith in the inherent goodness of the human spirit and the charitable value of giving to others. Her opinion comes from that foundation.

We talked on the phone once when she was in New York on leave. "If you are going to give," she said, "do it freely, from the heart. Don't try to control or influence. Give with an open hand."

I still haven't figured out if that was advice or admonishment.

It had a religious ring to it, but I wouldn't reject it on account of that.

Give with an open hand.

I liked it.

So that's what I'm doing.

12

Postscript No. 3 – 2011

At press time, Moammar Gadhafi is without a home. Who will take him?

Need you ask?

Mother Africa
The wrath of HIV
The shame of Apartheid
The dignity of Mama
The honesty of the Himba
The duplicity of the Namib
The rape of Zimbabwe
The pomp of the Zambezi
The lure of the Bush
The succor of Enjabulweni
The zeal of Melinda
The dream of Agnes
The conceit of Sanity
The gift of Perspective
Mother Africa

ABOUT THE AUTHOR

Phil Gray lives in Hawaii with his wife of many years. He has a law degree from Ohio State University and a certificate from Mt. Kilimanjaro National Park confirming he made it to the summit. He was active in the California and Hawaii real estate industry for more than 35 years. His wife says he is retired; he says he is on sabbatical.

CPSIA information can be obtained at www.ICGtesting.com
Printed in the USA
BVOW03s1014180214

345274BV00021B/610/P

9 781463 674359